ART   IDEAS   HISTORY

THE CRISIS
OF THE RENAISSANCE

1520-1600

ANDRÉ CHASTEL

TRANSLATED FROM THE FRENCH BY PETER PRICE

★

© 1968 by Editions d'Art Albert Skira, Geneva
Library of Congress Catalog Card Number: 68-20498.

★

Distributed in the United States by
THE WORLD PUBLISHING COMPANY
2231 West 110th Street, Cleveland, Ohio 44102

★

PRINTED IN SWITZERLAND

CONTENTS

JACOPO PONTORMO (1494-1557). THE HALBARDIER, 1530 OR 1537. CHAUNCEY STILLMAN COLLECTION, NEW YORK.

PASSION AND OSTENTATION

How confused is the Renaissance!... It stands hesitantly on the
threshold of a universe teeming with undreamed-of forms, ideas
and passions, as if an explorer were about to plunge into the virgin
forest of America, a labyrinth of innumerable trees and creepers
and strange plants, alive with the rustle of unknown creatures.

MICHELET, *The Renaissance*, XVII.

The character of the sixteenth century is dramatically and forcefully epitomized by the uneasy manner in which it drew to a close. The atmosphere was one of compromise, of policies dictated by circumspection and weariness. After fifty years of conflict, in which royal ambition had been constantly interwoven with religious strife, the monarchies of France and Spain had reached a balance of exhaustion. The new situation was marked, on the one hand, by Philip II's belated grant of freedom to the Protestant United Provinces, and on the other by the conversion of Henry of Navarre and the promulgation of the Edict of Nantes. Neither in politics, social questions nor religion had any movement remained intact or achieved its aims. For a long time the arts seemed preoccupied with renewing the experiences of that hectic age; yet they showed a curious dichotomy in which the contradictions of the century were endowed with poetic grandeur, while its excesses were denounced.

The greatest minds of the age set out to show how man was divided against himself. In the remorseless, strenuous, variegated world of Shakespeare, there was no room for a plain statement of life and passion. Cervantes, with the same concentrated admixture of commitment and irony, foretold that the romances of the past would live again in the novel. Montaigne, giving the signal for retreat, imbued philosophy with praise of reticence and silence. Bacon showed that exact learning must be revised from end to end.

Among painters, the aging El Greco in the solitude of Toledo and the youthful Caravaggio amid the bustle of Rome alike poured scorn on the mannered style then in vogue. Both upheld diversity of approach, laying the utmost emphasis on the contrasting principles of subjective vision and underlying "truth."

In every realm one finds a sort of irritable combativeness that was highly productive. The closing decade of the sixteenth century witnessed the muffled manifestoes of Giordano Bruno and the inspired pronouncements of Galileo, both placed under the ban of the Church. One has the impression of a great "isotherm," along which the noblest minds of the West twisted and turned as they wrestled to comprehend the conflicting elements of humanity.

Nothing was simple any more. Nothing was evident save the awareness of an indefeasible complexity more precious in the long run than the order, balance and reason on which men would always fix their hopes and for which they would always find stronger arguments. Everywhere they seemed to be more conscious of the price that must be paid for new-found truth, without in any way abating the prepossessions and emotions that ran counter to it. They grasped the ambiguity of man's condition in a manner that was deliberately challenging rather than pessimistic.

This may well give a first and vital clue to an understanding of the sixteenth century, for none of these attitudes would have been thinkable a century earlier, when Italy took the lead in that triumphant advance which may rightly be called the Renaissance. The problem here is to span this gap and discover what had happened since the days of Erasmus, Castiglione, Leonardo and Raphael. Considering the manner in which the century ended, how can one any longer maintain the traditional view of the Renaissance as a process of sustained development, as a steady ripening, interrupted only by fortuitous events? This interpretation may have appealed to those who were determined to make sense out of the farrago of history, by extracting from it only what might be said to favor the emergence of the "modern world." Bias of this sort would make an unfortunate beginning to a study of the originality of the Renaissance, and especially of the sixteenth century.

There was no rise followed by a decline, but rather one phase governed by optimism and dynamic aspirations, followed by another which saw that the first was over and drew the inevitable conclusions. After the flowering of the *myth of the Renaissance,* there arose a situation in which problems were so hydra-headed that the very magnitude of the effort put forth gave rise to the direst perplexities and dilemmas. The first phase may be dated from 1420 to 1520; the second, which concerns us here and which culminated in the *crisis of the Renaissance,* ran from the decade 1510-1520 to about 1600. Each period can only be fully appreciated in the light of the other, according to whether it is considered prophetically or in retrospect; both, however, are to some extent disparate and autonomous, in view of the nature and quantity of the phenomena that may be comprised within each.

During the first quarter of the sixteenth century one can point to the concomitance of various well-known events which show vividly how problems of every kind were suddenly speeded up. As a result the unity of Western civilization was to be endangered by a widening rift between the arts and the realities of political, religious and social life. Italy had become a bone of contention among the great powers. The French had devoted all their resources to her conquest under the leadership of their amazing king, Francis I, who sought to instil elegance and refinement into his uncouth nobility (an object for which in 1528 he was praised by Castiglione in the pages of *The Book of the Courtier*). In 1519, however, the imperial election conferred on the youthful Charles of Burgundy a tremendous inheritance of territory and traditions, enabling the House of Austria to take up the challenge of the French. By the time of Henry II the latter were compelled to accept the new balance of power embodied in the peace of Cateau-Cambrésis (1559), whereby most of Italy became a Spanish dependency. The machinations involved in these great upheavals gave rise to all sorts of political vagaries.

Thus some significance must be attached to Charles V's coronation at Bologna in 1530 and to the political climate it engendered. The ensuing struggle for power revived the concept of Empire and gave it portentous overtones that were at once classical (Rome), medieval (the Sword of State) and modern (universal authority). Yet the French were more in evidence than ever, and there is still some doubt as to the exact import and prospects of Francis I's candidature.

It was based on an ancient claim which reappeared in various unexpected guises. About 1523 "an anonymous writer produced a massive compilation, the *Mirabilis Liber*, of all the prophecies which from time immemorial beginning with Adso and the Sibyl of Tibur, had promised the Empire to the French. The latest of these prophecies, and the only recent one, foretold that in 1527 the last great monarch on earth, descended from the Kings of France, would come to Jerusalem, once more the seat of Papacy, to abdicate his throne" (Gaston Zeller, 1934).

The House of Spain was not to be outdone. In the fifteenth canto of *Orlando Furioso* a prophetess informs Astolfo that a Golden Age is to be ushered in by a prince "of the blood of Austria and Aragon." The poet "takes up the widely-held opinion that the discoveries (of the new world) were the harbinger of a new universal kingdom" (F. Yates, 1956).

The prevalence of such ideas is borne out by a mass of evidence, and one can hardly exaggerate the problems, hopes and fears conjured up by the spectacle of a colossus with one foot in the old world and one in a continent unknown to Antiquity. The whole axis of the West, which hitherto had lain principally on the Mediterranean, was shifting towards the Atlantic. Seville was rivaling Venice. Antwerp was eclipsing Milan and Rome. The scale of effective values had to be worked out afresh, a process that was to reverberate throughout the sixteenth century.

The field of investigation, discovery and conquest was now quite different from what it had been two or three generations earlier. The "discovery of Italy" had been accomplished; her humanists, craftsmen and diplomats were household names. Even the New World was losing its novelty. It had, so to speak, become part of the Old and was putting it out of joint, not only as a result of the gold of the Indies and the new trade-routes, but also in terms of intellectual inquiry and even of art. In 1521 the treasure of Montezuma was exhibited at Antwerp, where Dürer saw it. Exotic creatures like the parrot were all the rage and made their appearance in elegant portraits. There were even those who reflected on Man in a state of nature; for, despite the insane cruelty with which the Conquistadors brought the Gospel to their prey, people could not wholly ignore the claims of civilizations that were not Christian, or of a total paganism that defied the West. One soon encounters the apology of Las Casas and the speculative irony of Montaigne.

Much the same might be said of the Ottoman world and of the uneasy balance in the Mediterranean and Eastern Europe between the divided Powers of the West and the Empire which was the sworn enemy of Christendom. Throughout the fifteenth century Turkish power had expanded menacingly and a new situation arose when it was consolidated and the imperial capital of Stamboul began to flourish in the reign of Bayezid II.

Although the Ottomans were supposed to be the common adversary, they became more involved than ever in diplomatic chicanery. While fantastic tales were as numerous and as eagerly devoured as before, there was a great increase in more reliable information purveyed by travellers. One of the finest books of the period is the *Cosmographie du Levant* by André Thevet, published at Lyons in 1554 with woodcuts by Bernard Salomon, in which the vanished "wonders" of the ancient world appear beside the oddities of Asia.

The French incurred a good deal of rather disingenuous opprobrium when they sought in Suleyman the political and military counterpoise they needed to offset the power of the Empire. Already at the sea battle of Prevesa in 1538 a rather unedifying withdrawal on the part of the Christian squadrons commanded by Andrea Doria had revealed the reluctance both of the Venetians to work for Charles V and of Charles himself to do anything that might benefit Venice, the one Italian State that defied his authority. It was only after the loss of Cyprus, the last stronghold of the Venetian Republic in the Levant, that on the 7th of October 1571 the fleets of Christendom finally united against Turkey in the long-awaited victory of Lepanto. The tremendous impact of this event may be gauged from the number of allusions in contemporary literature and painting to the Church Triumphant and the discomfiture of the Infidel. And yet, two years later the Venetians, still and with good reason suspicious, signed a separate agreement with the Turks. It was yet another symptom of the "realism" and spirit of compromise that prevailed at the close of the century.

There was an even more tragic and categorical sense in which the Church was now confronted by new conditions. Before the *renovatio* the ambitions of ordinary men had been encouraged by ecclesiastics and humanists alike; now they were to culminate in the violent schism of the Reformation. The initiative passed to the Church in Northern Europe. Luther's nailing of his theses to the church door at Wittenberg in 1517 soon became something more than a local monastic squabble. The fateful intensifying of controversy was to be seen ten years later, when the German mercenaries of the Connétable de Bourbon sacked the Vatican as the Turks might have done and chastised the horrified city of Rome for the temerity of Pope Clement VII in thwarting the Emperor's will. The new intellectual centers of Basel and Geneva gave reality to this longitudinal division between North and South, which went far beyond religious matters and pervaded every aspect of behavior, social conventions and the arts. After the 1520s the sixteenth century entered on a phase of unremitting strain and insecurity which destroyed illusions and brought in its wake an almost unbearable succession of bloodshed and holocaust, of hopes and follies. Some of its consequences will be considered shortly.

What is one to say of what has been called the "third force," the active historical factor of Humanism, which had come to bulk so large in Western Europe? By means of the printed and spoken word it had given a great impetus to civilization; yet it has always been held partly responsible for the schism that tore the West asunder. On the one hand, Humanism reached a point where it stagnated as a result of over-specialization and technical minutiae. It became bogged down in formal argument and pedantic bickering, to which even such men as Erasmus or Henri Estienne were not immune. Learning and scholarship made noteworthy gains, but in a haphazard, incoherent manner that should not be overlooked, for it resulted in some rather disconcerting affinities.

On the other hand, Humanism underwent a phase of crisis whose features are worth examining and can, in fact, be summed up in a single phrase: the *crisis of the Renaissance*. This idea connotes not only the many achievements of the recent past but the oppressive sense of a present harassed by tragic dilemmas and unforeseen contingencies. There were many gains to record: men of genius had emerged; manners were changing and the courtly style had taken shape; literary standards had been or were being set up; technical mastery had been won. Yet in every domain men were being overtaken by events and were constantly forced to adjust themselves to problems which they could not master.

In a situation so rich in promise and so fraught with peril one finds a number of salient ethical features that ought to be stated at the outset in order to portray the new age, albeit a little artificially. One of these features is the triumph of *ostentation* over many public and private virtues. Another is the growing influence of *passion* over the lives of men and women. They constitute two facets of a rule of conduct utterly divorced from that spirit of rational orderliness and personal restraint which had marked the previous phase but which from now on is hardly characteristic of the century.

The most revealing side of human behavior is, perhaps, to be inferred from economic facts. Ethically, the Humanists who followed Erasmus, and in terms of "sociology" historians such as Guicciardini, were among the first writers to perceive the deeper implications of material wealth. The most casual observer of this period cannot fail to be struck by the conflict between rich and poor, between the fat kine and the lean, or by the influence of wealthy patrons and the sharp setbacks caused by economic depression. The prosperity of France and her concomitant expansion were major factors until about the middle of the century. The appearance of a financial caste in States that were beginning to centralize their government led to rivalry between a middle class relying on powerful cities and an aristocracy whose authority was still rooted in its broad acres. While progress in architecture was due to the urban plutocracy and to the affluence of "feudal" families (whether old or recent), it also owed something to the need for *display*. Throughout the States of Europe the same phenomenon was apparent: great banking and commercial houses

at the service of princes who could only manifest their sovereignty by pouring out money on magnificence. In the case of Charles V and Francis I, of Henry VIII and great Roman families like the Borghese, not to mention the last Valois kings and Emperor Rudolph II at Prague, financiers provided cash for the most spendthrift governments the world had ever known.

The rise of capitalism, fed by gold from the Indies and stimulated by the mercantile cities of Northern Europe, was indeed a cardinal factor, with many ramifications; but it should not be allowed to overshadow another important factor, one which not only corroborates the first but points to some of its deeper implications. Society in those days was still based as much on *rank* and *service* as on competition and profit. The former were so closely bound up with economic activity and played so frequent a part in public crises that the historian should beware of treating them as if they were spurious or of small account. Where one finds evidence of a characteristic impulse, a sort of general propensity shared by city-states and monarchies, by townsfolk and nobles, it may for convenience sake be described as *ostentation*.

There is, however, a cognate circumstance, less easily apprehended by the modern mind familiar with investment and profitability: namely the sheer volume of useless expenditure, the part played by spectacular waste and, above all, the kind of obligation that made such things necessary.

Princely munificence and power were never so evident as in the awarding of titles and benefices, with their attendant perquisites. Such things were universally coveted, and few were ashamed to solicit them or to lavish praises on the royal benefactor. There are a hundred examples, comic or painful, in English, Spanish, Italian literature. It was for this purpose that Ronsard revived the art of panegyric; and as for that arch-blackmailer and formidable tuft-hunter, Aretino, his eternal cadging, far from causing offence, merely gave rise to apprehension among those who did not requite it. Titian, the greatest of Venetian painters, had also the keenest nose for a patron. Vasari, in his fresco of 1546 in the chancellery in Rome, saw fit to portray Paul III exercising his most august prerogative in the ceremonial distribution of endowments.

Many were the consequences that flowed from these ideas. Power, whatever its nature, legitimate or disputed, stable or precarious, required display. In those days a prince only carried conviction when he succeeded in arousing astonishment and delight. The court by which he must be surrounded and its punctilio, which was beginning to be formulated, provided a sumptuous show for the benefit not only of the high and mighty but also of the common herd, who expected their masters to act the part. When Cardinal Alessandro Farnese became Paul III, the palace designed by Sangallo, which seemed good enough for a cardinal, would not do for a pope. The same was true of interior decoration, with the result that artists were always being called upon to meet the demand for grandeur. It was not so much a matter of "cultural policy" as of status symbols.

The word " Court " may be said to designate the frame constructed around a prince to serve his purposes and reflect his personality. Kings like Francis I, Henry VIII and Philip II are inseparable from their frames. The sixteenth century was the age in which the professional courtier was born and flourished.

It was only natural that court life, originating with the monarch and aping his tastes, should also become a major civilizing influence; for poets, humanists and scholars, as well as most artists, usually served some prince as secretaries, "orators," agents or often as purely nominal administrators. Such men were Budé, Ronsard, Philibert Delorme, Benvenuto Cellini. This process of "attachment" was what caused thinkers and creative spirits to be constantly on the look-out for patrons. It also meant, however, that while the protagonists of culture found themselves drawn into the narrow orbit fixed by the character and fortunes of kings, the latter, too, underwent the counter-attraction of an influence transcending their own. There was nothing new about this, but it became more and more significant as the trend spread farther, from middleclass townsfolk to feudal nobility, from Flanders and the Rhine to Rome and Florence. Owing to various factors—the flourishing side by side of mercantile cities and princely courts, the rivalry of North and South, the general code of behavior—the sixteenth century was characterized to a quite unusual degree by desires and motives of this kind.

This is best evidenced by the unprecedented proliferation of *pageantry,* both as a royal amusement round which court life revolved, as a raree-show for the masses and as the indispensable ratification of power. We shall later examine the many ways in which art and society became closely associated in the ephemeral and spectacular. Another, less familiar aspect of social ostentation may be seen in the craze, common to Italian and Transalpine cities, for *painted façades.* It showed both the strong proclivity towards make-believe and the way in which art had, as it were, come down to street-level. In its new-found popularity this ancient, rather naïve practice had given itself airs and assumed a curiously histrionic attitude, in the form of a striking desire to "illustrate" architecture. If our analysis is correct as regards economic and social practice, it shows that a strong element of aberration existed in both forms of behavior, which in other respects seemed usually to have been governed by the profit motive and practical considerations. In this respect the relationship between logic and real life took an unusual twist.

This can be seen in individual behavior, which in general was undeniably prone to be governed by emotive and irrational forces. One can, of course, adopt Michelet's and Burckhardt's view of the Renaissance as "man's self-discovery and emancipation," which was certainly a cardinal feature of the "myth" of rebirth and renewal. But at the time with which we are concerned the desire for *prestige* had become a driving force that was to have momentous consequences. It gave an exhibitionist quality to men's self-consciousness and urged them to assert themselves more emphatically than ever. People from the most varied walks of life tended more and more to become excitable, hysterical, boisterous and wildly impulsive. One could almost sum up the Renaissance in the days of Henry VIII, Philip II and Charles IX by modifying the classical definition into "a discovery of the truth and fertility of man's emotions."

This is borne out by the most convincing examples, for the sixteenth century was a golden age of ferocity, bloodshed, violence and vendetta. One need only recall the sack of Rome, the sanguinary Peasants' Revolt in Germany, the carnage wrought by the Duke of Alva in the Netherlands, the Massacre of St Bartholomew, all the noble assassins and noble victims who set the tone for the age. The same sort of thing can be found in the world of thought and ethics; witness Luther, Ignatius of Loyola, Calvin, Michael Servetus, Agrippa d'Aubigné or, on a different plane, the example of *terribilità* given by Michelangelo. Character had ceased to be the expression of a man's inner self; it consisted wholly in the energy with which he fulfilled himself unrestrainedly. Sometimes, of course, he had to dismount from his high horse, and there would be frequent crises, sudden retreats and unexpected reversals.

There is no denying that Symonds, Nietzsche and Taine were right to be impressed by this unbridled vitality. Yet if one glances at the memoirs or diaries of the time one is struck by the impersonal quality of these private jottings. As Lucien Febvre has rightly pointed out, one cannot extract from Marguerite de Navarre the hidden meanings that connoisseurs of confessions and introspection are wont to discover in Jean-Jacques Rousseau. If romanticism connotes emotional depths and preoccupation with the inner self, no age was ever less romantic than the sixteenth century. Its whole dynamism was one of tension, appetite and the will to succeed. This may have been due to a weakening in the educative power of humanism. Formerly the inner man had been, as it were, regulated by the authority of classical and Christian precepts, which laid down the great ideal "forms" of human nature—nobility, heroism, saintliness; now, however, neither clerks nor barons found them wholly adequate. One can feel the slackening of these standards as one progresses from Erasmus to Amyot and then to Montaigne, or compares the chivalry of Ariosto, still so ingenuous at heart, with the complex morality of Shakespeare's noblest characters. The universal success of Castiglione's *Book of the Courtier,* as popular in France and Spain as it was in Italy, shows how completely values had become "social." It is true that men like Ignatius of Loyola and Melanchthon tried to indicate a new approach to religious instruction; but as regards the sum of human ethics no one saw deeper into men's hearts than Shakespeare or Cervantes. One of the paradoxes of the sixteenth century is that it inveigles the historian into becoming a biographer and tempts him to construct one of those portrait galleries that were becoming so popular in the palaces and mansions of the time. The fact is, however, that straightforward psychology does not really hold the key to this garrulous, complicated, extrovert age. It is rather by comparing the first trait we emphasized, *ostentation,* with the sovereign influence of *passion* that one can most clearly grasp why the outcome of the Renaissance was not an advance in the art of history or biography, but a magnificent flowering of the theater in England, of the opera in Italy and of the festal spirit generally.

1

PAINTED FAÇADES

Prestige and display: on these both princes and merchants of the Renaissance set great store and they were powerful factors in molding the features of both palaces and cities; their effects can be observed in Flanders, on the Rhine, in Rome, Venice and Prague.

A society in which such factors counted for so much is very inadequately described by modern terms like "showy" or "luxury-loving." The concentration of wealth in the commercial towns and at the courts, acted on by the stimulus of competition between North and South, gave rise throughout the sixteenth century to a wide variety of manifestations. The ardor with which the new style of Renaissance art was applied to festival scenery, to ceremonial and costume, tends to make us forget that these were but latter-day variations on practices that were already centuries-old.

But pageantry and festivities had come to play a larger part in social life than ever before. They gave an attractive décor to the street and all that went on in the street, the more so since, whether religious or secular, or both at once, they played up the temporary and the marvelous at the expense of the humdrum and the everyday. They reacted on art in many ways, and one of the least noticed, yet most revealing aspects of social ostentation is to be found in the vogue for painted façades.

...FUMI (1486-1551).
...A HOUSE FRONT. UNDATED.
...WINDSOR CASTLE.
...HER MAJESTY THE QUEEN.

LELIO ORSI (1511-1587). DESIGN FOR THE FAÇADE DECORATION OF HIS OWN HOUSE.
UNDATED. PEN AND BROWN BRUSH HEIGHTENED WITH WHITE.
DEVONSHIRE COLLECTION, CHATSWORTH. BY COURTESY OF THE TRUSTEES OF THE CHATSWORTH SETTLEMENT.

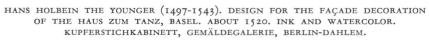

HANS HOLBEIN THE YOUNGER (1497-1543). DESIGN FOR THE FAÇADE DECORATION
OF THE HAUS ZUM TANZ, BASEL. ABOUT 1520. INK AND WATERCOLOR.
KUPFERSTICHKABINETT, GEMÄLDEGALERIE, BERLIN-DAHLEM.

It was common practice in the Middle Ages to adorn a house front or the façade of a public building with a fresco representing a coat of arms on a pious figure. But the extension of the painting to the entire façade, thus forming with the doors and bays a studied whole taking the place of ornamental sculpture, does not seem to have occurred until the end of the fifteenth century.

Early examples of painted façades are known both north and south of the Alps, and in Switzerland, Austria, North Italy and also the Carpathians (where they have a distinctly eastern flavor) these decorative paintings long continued to be made. Many such, as colorful as peasant costumes, can still be seen on house and church fronts in these regions. It would be rash, however, to suppose that they either originated in the Balkans or were peculiar to mountain peoples.

In fact one of the places where this type of decoration first appears is Rome. There, on the initiative of Peruzzi, a palace front was decorated with a monochrome painting at the beginning of the sixteenth century: traces of it have been found on the garden façade of the Farnesina. From the second quarter of the century on, many palace fronts were adorned with "heroic" friezes marking off one storey from another and comprising simulated niches with figures of heroes and emperors. Maccari noted in the 1880s some of the most remarkable examples which, like the frescoes of the Palazzo Milesi by Polidoro and Maturino, have sadly deteriorated since then. Less spectacular are the ornamental arabesques and *sgraffiti* on patrician houses in Central Italy; often these are set off by bosses or nail-headed moldings, following a practice that reappears as far away as Moscow and Zagorsk in the eighteenth century. The principle behind this decoration is the association, peculiar to the Renaissance, of antique themes (substituted for heraldic motifs) and illusionist or *trompe-l'œil* effects (replacing modest panels of color). The fashion now was all for arches of triumph, for festal *apparati*, for houses whose street fronts were bright with painted figures.

This was the fashion followed by Holbein in the dazzling decorations he devised for the Haus zum Tanz in the Eisengasse at Basel. He emphasized their theatrical illusionism with irresistible brio by "hollowing" the façade with galleries where a fantastic spectacle is taking place—in effect an alluring invitation to turbulence and pleasure. At about the same time the Sienese master Beccafumi was devising a scheme of niches and moldings which provided a setting on the façade for his elevating allegories but which ignored the actual structure of the building. From then on, the painted façade became an open field for the entertaining or provocative imaginings of the Mannerist decorators. Many of them seem to have entered that field with the sole purpose of drawing attention to their own houses.

Lelio Orsi, for example. His façade decoration, which has survived only in the sumptuous sketches he prepared for it, included, besides his "signature" in the guise of some bear cubs (*orsi* in Italian meaning bears), the figure of an archer about to let fly an arrow straight at the spectator.

Thus the pompous style of the Renaissance ended up in claptrap and exhibitionism. The architecture itself was completely lost sight of: it became a mere support for eye-catching imagery, and as such it had a stimulating effect on peasant art. But at the level of the bourgeoisie and the nobility the function of the façade as a medium of display and swagger is only too apparent in Dietterlin's elaborate patterns of arches, supports and bays. His *Architectura* (1598) offers a whole repertory of doorways and façades in which all the structural elements, treated as living forms, are combined in a showy demonstrativeness whose fascination is undeniable.

WENDEL DIETTERLIN. FAÇADE DESIGN.
PLATE 29 FROM HIS "DE ARCHITECTURA," NUREMBERG 1598.
BIBLIOTECA CANTONALE, LUGANO.

WENDEL DIETTERLIN. DESIGN FOR A PORTAL.
PLATE 24 FROM HIS "DE ARCHITECTURA," NUREMBERG 1598.
BIBLIOTECA CANTONALE, LUGANO

CHIAROSCURO CELEBRE ESISTENTE IN ROMA IN VIA DELLA MASCHERA D'ORO N.7
Opera di Maturino Fiorentino e di Polidoro da Caravaggio

POLIDORO DA CARAVAGGIO (1500-1546) AND MATURINO DA FIRENZE (1490-1528).
FAÇADE PAINTING OF THE PALAZZO MILESI, ROME. PLATE 38 FROM ENRICO MACCARI, "GRAFFITI E CHIAROSCURI
ALL'ESTERNO DELLE CASE," 1885. MUSEO DI ROMA, ROME.

I

IMAGE AND SPEECH

ANTHONIS MOR (1519-ABOUT 1576). PORTRAIT OF ANTOINE PERRENOT DE GRANVELLA, 1549.
KUNSTHISTORISCHES MUSEUM, VIENNA.

THE AWARENESS OF EXISTENCE

The sheer loquacity of the Renaissance is staggering. In 1499 when that strange work, the *Dream of Polyphilus,* written in a polyglot travesty of Italian, was printed by Aldus Manutius, it fell flat; for that was the age of the purists, of Bembo and the disciples of Politian. Fifty years later, however, with the appearance in 1545 of a new Venetian edition and in 1546 of a French translation by Jean Martin (who boasted that he had "done his utmost to render a more than Asiatic prolixity with a French conciseness that would give general satisfaction"), Colonna's cloudy, high-flown *magnum opus* acquired real significance.

The *Dream of Polyphilus* may be regarded as one of the key works in the European literature of this period. Written for a readership with a smattering of humanism, it was a new version, paganized, sensual, colorful, of the *Roman de la Rose*; the initiation into the rites of love is so thoroughly allegorical that almost any meaning can be read into it (later it was even imagined that the secrets of alchemy could be gleaned from it). Not only a quarry of allegorical themes, it is also a repertory of architectonic forms, of model inscriptions, of picture puzzles. All the arts readily found in it something to their purpose. The Renaissance expected a book to contain a wealth of connotations, but few can show a happier blend of typography and illustrations. And few exemplify so strikingly the new taste for devious and suggestive language, rich in overtones. The narrative is deliberately presented as a series of objects and scenes. Most of the imaginative literature of the Renaissance relies on the author's power of description, on *ekphrasis*, and there was a steady demand for the Alexandrian and Roman writers who provided the model for it; hence the many editions of Philostratus and Ovid, among others. But the writer, or adaptor, of such literature was drawn on and on, irresistibly, in a striving after verbal effects: the result was a relentless torrent of phrases and epithets, as if, in his effort to encompass and render this new world, the writer had become word-drunk.

It is a remarkable fact that the verbal luxuriance of the *Dream of Polyphilus* reacted not only on the style of comedy writing and the language of poetry, but even on the phraseology of learned writers. In France, to take a trivial but symptomatic example, the macaronic verse of Merlo Coccaie exploited the comic possibilities of jargon well before Rabelais' *écolier limousin*. But Rabelais took to juggling and clowning with words on a colossal scale. New coinages and remoldings of style and vocabulary were recognized as the poet's privilege, and it was freely exercised by Ronsard, Philip Sidney and Tasso; each developed an elaborate syntax whose shining coils glittered with etymological arabesques. Shakespeare inherited this tradition, and his amazing style was enriched by a torrent of strange words, startling images, echoes and repetitions that delighted the poets and courtiers of Europe. These excesses gave rise to feelings of distrust. Petrus Ramus, for instance, wanted to reform the structure of a language whose vocabulary had run riot. Bonaventure des Périers and Robert Estienne saw it as a vehicle for dangerous hyperbole. Montaigne believed that it lent itself to lying and vapidity. Characters who used their gift of the gab so freely sometimes found themselves brought up short:

> Words are grown so false
> I am loath to prove reason with them.
>
> (*Twelfth Night*, III, i)

The concern with words and their misuse shown by thoughtful men of this period is probably connected with the religious crisis. The characteristic development of literature outlined above has its parallel, moreover, in the arts. The clear-cut phrasing of Calvin and the rugged verve of Luther practically founded the public press in French and German, through both their polemical writings and their translations of Scripture. The great English translations of the Bible marked a decisive step in the molding of English speech and culture; the names and doings of the Israelites were made familiar to all, and generations have been nourished on the Prayer Book and the Bible. Things never went so far in France, not even in the most liberal phase of the Reformation. Apart from their psalms and church music, the Huguenots had no style of their own. But the French Protestants, as a minority in revolt, do sometimes show a lucidity and a critical acumen which give their best letter-writers and chroniclers a distinctive sobriety and simplicity of language. "It is a striking fact that among the papists we find only mediocre annalists, like Beaucaire or Belleforest, or bigoted ranters like Sorlin and Claude de Sainctes. The talent and historical sense are on the Protestant side with de Serres or d'Aubigné" (H. Hauser). This may be overstating the case a little, particularly as regards d'Aubigné, who took a very lofty view of history and never wrote a line dispassionately. The moral dignity of a great many spokesmen of embattled Protestantism, and the tone it gives their writings, is nevertheless a fact, and a significant one.

Far from being diffuse or bizarre, their style is often crisp. In the mordant dialectic of Calvin, the words owe much of their force to the rigor of the syntax: *"Quelle chose convient mieux à la foi que de nous reconnaître nus de toute vertu pour être vêtus de Dieu? Vidés de tout bien pour être remplis de lui? Serfs du péché pour être délivrés…? C'est icelle grâce seule, laquelle induit nos cœurs à suivre son mouvement et y produit tant l'élection que la volonté, tellement que toutes bonnes œuvres qui s'inscrivent après sont fruits d'icelle, et n'est point reçu d'homme vivant sinon d'autant qu'elle a formé son cœur à l'obéissance"* (Institution Chrétienne, I). But this is a highly personal example. Intent as they were on capturing the imagination by extracting from the Bible all that is vivid and colorful, the Huguenots might have been expected to make the most of dramatic unity and invoke the famous *Abraham sacrifiant* of Théodore de Bèze (1550). But the movement in this direction never went far, and the countless transpositions of the story of Daniel or David show no natural leaning towards "classicism."

There was no place for such simplifications in the literary ferment of the time. To find in the Renaissance drama a certain firmness of style and language, we have to turn from the great names to such men as Jodelle or Jacques Grévin, who was associated for a time with Ronsard. The drama, whether Catholic or Protestant, had no use for concentration or purity of line. The vogue for Seneca, so widespread that even the Jesuits gave way to it, points clearly enough to its main features: tearful melodrama, headlong passion, wordy speechifying, and extreme situations culminating in the hero's resounding triumph or utter downfall.

The tireless reiteration of commonplaces is equally characteristic of this literature and, under cover of gnomic turns of phrase and mythological allusions, of a habit of mind which seems to find in them a perennial appeal. The writer's aim is not so much a clarity as a plethora of expression. His right to borrow from others, freely and abundantly, was taken for granted. Joachim Du Bellay could say without compunction: "I pride myself on having invented what I have translated word for word from others." This is particularly true of the shorter pieces and divertissements in his *Jeux Rustiques* published in 1558. "The fact that these works are translations cannot detract from the genuine pleasure they give, nor from the genuine feeling for nature which comes through so vividly in some of these charming pieces" (V. L. Saulnier). The literature of the present grows out of the literature of the past, and these exercises in translation and adaptation, so remarkable in their scope and variety, were a necessary stimulus. But not for a long time was it realized that exuberance of language is incompatible with refinement of language. Everywhere in the West writers let themselves be carried away by words. The effects in poetry, as in art, were being felt acutely in the last third of the sixteenth century. To keep to the example of French literature, the demands made on words took two characteristic forms: a certain torsion, as in the sonnets of Jean de Sponde, with their continual twists and turns around recurring, image-bearing words; and a torrential outpouring of words, as in the *Sepmaine* of Guillaume Du Bartas. One puzzles and teases the reader, the other overwhelms him.

From the subtlest distinctions to the most out-spoken blasts of vulgarity, there was nothing the men of the sixteenth century did not try to put into words. A great part of their vast literary output consisted of tales, chronicles and memoirs—much of it now unreadable. A distinguished commander, Monluc, left a minute and boring description of his campaigns. That turbulent but gifted craftsman, Cellini, devoted the clouded evening of his life to composing, under the eye of the Florentine police, his interminable but highly entertaining memoirs. They all took the great table-talkers of antiquity as their model and set themselves to build up a fund of good stories. Some, like the worthy Etienne Pasquier, practically made this their life's work. Brantôme, the chattiest and most trivial of them all, wrote lives of famous men and his collection of dirty stories about wanton women, based on the gossip and tattle with which a practised memory and roving eye supplied him.

Who were the men who produced such stuff—tale-bearers, paid hacks, failures trying to get their own back? To some extent, perhaps. But the fact remains that most of these amateur historians were obeying the compulsive urge of that garrulous age to *talk* about life in all its aspects, from the significant to the inane. There is something disconcerting about the lack of proportion in these pseudo-biographers and pseudo-historians, who aped only too successfully one of the worst features of Greek and Roman literature, its fondness for anecdotes and tall stories.

Men like Bonaventure des Périers and Robert Etienne renewed the attempts made by certain Italian critics in the previous century to counteract such pinchbeck imitation. They tried to expose its falseness, but their scholarly admonitions went unheeded. The fashion was for the tales of *Amadis,* the "lives" of Plutarch, interminable romances and chronicles stuffed with naïve bragging and derring-do, which were to provide grist to Cervantes' mill. No one was more sceptical of this tendency than Montaigne, who had given much thought to it. Yet he, too, adopted the pantechnicon method, for there does not appear to have been any really objective standard of judgment. It was all very well to laugh at the romance-mongers, but one must not

ignore the views of "ordinary folk, who had nothing of their own to offer and could only contribute a careful and diligent compendium of everything that came to their notice, setting it down conscientiously and without picking or choosing" (Montaigne's Essays, II, 10).

No picking or choosing: that is the heart of the matter. Shakespeare often gives the impression that he does not intend to let anything escape him. Everyone must be dragged in, and the clash of contrasts, which so delighted the Romantics (and sometimes led them astray), is one aspect of that principle of alternating viewpoints which governed the composition as a whole. The grave-digger, the drunken trooper, the sailor, the ruffian, and of course the fool with his unlicensed speech, intervene to make it clear that every situation can be seen and appreciated from quite a different angle from that of prince, hero or lover. Their talk, in its color and variety, gives us a sense of that many-sided richness of life which it is neither possible nor desirable to refine away. The same instinct is at work in Bruegel and Tintoretto, with their genius for depicting "the mutable, rank-scented many." The result was a curious lack of what would be known nowadays as psychology. The individual revealed himself through his acts and movements; but he only did so in the context of cut-and-dried, stereotyped situations, and one must therefore investigate the way in which these definitions were applied by writers and artists.

The keynote was always determined by the narrative itself. It was only possible for Vasari, the historian of Italian art, to portray his subjects in the form of chronicles enlivened by anecdotes; they were men busied with their affairs, not rapt in silent introspection. (It was a remarkable and widely admired feat that Vasari managed by such means to formulate a general aesthetic theory.) To revert once more to Montaigne—and bearing in mind that his was an exceptional case—he did indeed attempt and achieve the total awareness that his contempories eschewed; but he approached his goal along the highways and byways of wide reading and the discursive essay. In other words he, too, followed a path dictated by the association of ideas and the meandering of an unplanned soliloquy.

THE PORTRAIT

The sixteenth century is so rich in portraiture that few periods appear so familiar to us. It was then that this form of art, already practised very widely, was organized and developed on an almost industrial scale. The mode was already well established, but now it was no longer a case, as it once had been, of merely depicting the donor of an altarpiece or a prince surrounded by his household. Beginning with Francis I, the iconography of French kings acquired ritual significance, and their thirst for prestige may be seen in the frequent commissions given to the Italian masters and their pupils or to Flemish painters like Joos van Cleve. Charles V took up the French challenge by patronizing Titian. Holbein embarked on the career of a professional portraitist that finally led him to settle in London from 1532, where he painted Henry VIII in many different attitudes. The Elector of Saxony found his Titian in Lucas Cranach. In addition to the State portrait there grew up at the French court, around 1500, the attractive habit of doing three-color portraits, in red, black and white chalk. Throughout the sixteenth century the immensely prolific Clouets, father and son, followed by Dumonstier and others, executed a great range of likenesses, subtle, persuasive and only unequal in so far as there were many copies and repetitions. The robust Holbein was not so successful in setting a fashion. The line-drawing led naturally to the small painting or miniature, faithfully echoed in the Princesse de Clèves *by the charming incident of the stolen portrait, which took place in the reign of Henry II.*

We have begun with court portraits and the predilections of the nobility because they had so great an influence on art trends. Practically every major artist of the sixteenth century exercised his talents in this way, and some of them did almost nothing else. There was Bronzino at Florence. There was Anthonis Mor from Antwerp, who worked at Madrid under the name of Antonio Moro and there popularized the Italian grand manner with excellent taste and considerable skill. Artists who struck medals and sculpted busts were equally numerous, and their influence extended from Germany to Italy. Leone Leoni, followed by his son Pompeo, seems to have made bronzes of the entire imperial family.

In Flanders it had long been customary for merchants to hang pictures of themselves in their homes. The portrait, which up to the 1530s had been something of a luxury, began to be enjoyed by scholars, churchmen and the middle classes. Artists themselves caught the prevailing mood, with the result that self-portraits abounded, the new manner branched forth in many directions and the sixteenth century became a sort of hall of mirrors. It is hardly surprising that an age which so lavishly depicted the features and attitudes of men and women should be credited, rightly or wrongly, with having invented "character."

The portrait was always engendered by the fusion of a fixed social convention (the subject must be unmistakably defined) with a variable artistic convention (according to whether the painter employed a reach-me-down style or did his sitter the honor of devising a new one for him). One is struck by the immense variety of attitudes, for the range of "types"—heroic, aristocratic, lonely—was extensive both for noblemen and their ladies. The general trend of the period is most clearly revealed by the success of Parmigianino's "fashion plates." The different styles of portraiture were clearly calculated to bring out the aspects of passion —or, for that matter, of lordly reserve—that determined the sitter's character. It would seem that the painter was sometimes trying to capture the very essence of his subject's life. This may account for some of the finest and most endearing portraits of lovers and patrons of the arts that have ever been painted. There had never been anything in painting comparable to the couples portrayed by Lotto, in a cold range of colors, and by Titian, in rich warm tones; to the admirable Andrea Odoni *of the first, chilly and sensitive, and the noble and masterly* Jacopo de Strada *of the second.*

After Leonardo, Raphael, Holbein and the early Titian, painting had virtually mastered the process of reproducing a man's countenance in terms of his character and immediate surroundings—atmosphere or domestic interior. Portraiture no longer presented any serious technical difficulties and had become purely a matter of style. Never had there been such sharp divarications of manner as among the successors of Raphael and Leonardo. Max Friedländer has admirably described Titian "painting without any preliminary sketch, but seizing form and color at a glance; Holbein on the other hand, giving form and color a crystalline fixity, regardless of the contingencies of light and setting." Contrary to the common assertion about national aptitudes, it is the southerner who captures the momentary vision and seems more true to life, the northerner who creates the lasting image.

Apart from this noteworthy contrast between the great masters, the sixteenth century witnessed an astonishing quest for elegance. Beginning with Bronzino, and especially Parmigianino, portraiture acquired a wonderful degree of sophistication. It went beyond the mere statement of personality and definition of social or professional status; rather it sought to create a definitive model, something that could only be achieved on the basis of a strong graphic tradition. This polishing of an already established form and style is characteristic of Mannerism. Portraits became arbitrary, allusive, allegorical, formal even as a coat of arms. This was the main objective of painters, from Fontainebleau to Prague. The stiff, beruffed miniatures of Hilliard, Holbein's unlikely successor, were all the rage at the court of Queen Elizabeth.

FRANCIABIGIO (1482-1525). PORTRAIT OF A STUDENT AT HIS DESK, 1522.
STAATLICHE MUSEEN, BERLIN. GEMÄLDEGALERIE, DAHLEM.

SEBASTIANO DEL PIOMBO (1485-1547). BUST PORTRAIT OF A MAN IN ARMOR, ABOUT 1516-1518.
WADSWORTH ATHENEUM, HARTFORD, CONN.

LORENZO LOTTO (ABOUT 1480-1556). PORTRAIT OF ANDREA ODONI, 1527. HAMPTON COURT.
REPRODUCED BY GRACIOUS PERMISSION OF HER MAJESTY THE QUEEN. COPYRIGHT RESERVED.

TITIANVS · F

IACOBVS · DE
NIS · ROMANV
TIQVARIVS · E
AN · AE

Cr. R. 6

TITIAN (ABOUT 1489/1490-1576). PORTRAIT OF JACOPO DE STRADA, 1567-1568.
KUNSTHISTORISCHES MUSEUM, VIENNA.

Cr. R. 7

LEONE LEONI (ABOUT 1509-1590) AND POMPEO LEONI (1533-1608). TOMB OF CHARLES V (DETAIL), 1593.
BRONZE. CHURCH OF THE ESCORIAL.

32

GERMAIN PILON (ABOUT 1537-1590) IN COLLABORATION WITH HIS SON RAPHAËL. RENÉ DE BIRAGUE, CHANCELLOR OF FRANCE (DETAIL), 1584-1585. BRONZE. LOUVRE, PARIS.

SIGHT AND HEARING

In those days it was the fashion for every man of noble or gentle birth to wear on the brim of his hat a little gold medal inscribed with a motto or some such conceit.

CELLINI, *Memoirs*, I, 6.

According to Lucien Febvre, there is a danger, not so much of exaggerating the dynamism and passion of an age, but rather of overlooking its mental properties and the way in which its intellectual ferment and sensibility found expression. It is as well to begin by examining the clearest evidence. We are, indeed, compelled to do so by reason of a strange and egregious error on the part of this distinguished historian, although there is some justification for it in the fact that he was writing mainly in a French context. To him, the men of the Renaissance were governed much more by *hearing* than by sight, and this imbalance of the senses would account in part for the intensity of their emotional reactions. We have already seen how the sixteenth century was more addicted to narrative than to description. The pages of Du Bellay, Monluc and Brantôme abound in quotations, and every remark is recorded; but there is never a "silhouette" or a visual symbol, so one is forced to conclude that the shocks of sensibility were conveyed by ear, or even by touch.

It was, of course, an age much given to singing. Marot's setting of the Psalms, like the *Odes* which Ronsard later composed to be sung, created a minor revolution. The Reformation drew support from this common disposition. Bernard Palissy, in a passage which pleased Michelet, describes the impact of church reform at Saintes, in southwestern France. "You might have seen, of a Sunday, the journeymen out for a walk in the grasslands and copses, whole groups of them singing together the psalms and canticles. You might have seen the maids, sitting in the gardens, taking delight in singing together to the glory of God." Luther turned this disposition to account, and Geneva even more so: the *Psalmier complet* of Théodore de Bèze (1562), set to music by Goudimel, marks the peak

of this trend. Music was no less closely bound up with secular life and the pleasures of the court. It was a mighty instrument of persuasion in the hands of the Counter-Reformation; think of Monteverdi, Palestrina, the Venetian organists. Everywhere there was an outburst of song, of melodies that seem to us so tremulous and delicate, for the great innovations did not take place till the end of the century. Music played a notable part in the arts. The sixteenth century opened with the meditative tone of Giorgione's *Concert*, which was completed by Titian; and it is the harpsichord player who enhances the beauty and poetic feeling of the Prado *Venus*. Pictures were full of concerts, musical instruments, and singers, and one associates certain sound effects with certain painters—the raucous clamor of Giulio Romano and Rosso, the guffaws of Bruegel, the speaking gestures, shouts and sighs of Primaticcio and Niccolò dell'Abbate. It was a noisy age, constantly assaulting the eyes and ears.

This point, however, cannot be accepted without considering another of equal significance. It would seem that the Renaissance was incapable of expressing even the most tangible forms of emotional satisfaction without relating them to music. For Clément Marot, who translated the Psalms into French, the mystical yearning of the hymns was inseparable from the music they are sung to:

> *Ce n'est qu'amour. Amour luy-même*
> *Par sa sapience supreme*
> *Les composa...*
>
> (*Epître aux Dames de France*, 1543)

Musical theory must have had immense influence, slightly mitigated, perhaps, by the triteness with which it was sometimes expressed. From the Quattrocento on, the Neo-Platonism of the *Timaeus*, combined with a certain "Orphic" tradition, regarded the musical scale as, in a sense, reflecting the properties of the cosmos and as being the point of fusion between man's soul and his physical environment.

A case in point was Francesco Giorgi's *De harmonia mundi totius* published at Venice in 1525. He used Pythagorean philosophy and a cabbalistic interpretation of Holy Writ to erect a system which he claimed to be a general Open Sesame. This writer is of some interest to historians because in 1534 he was asked to comment on Jacopo Sansovino's design for the church of San Francesco della Vigna. His paper clearly illustrates a certain approach to the study of architectural proportions, and the conclusions he drew were submitted to Serlio and Titian. The connection is certainly interesting; but it only goes to show that, while music enjoyed a kind of theoretical preponderance, this did not amount to pre-eminence among the arts.

The point calls for closer examination, based on this same instance. Giorgi's treatise had a great success in France, where Guy Le Fèvre de la Boderie translated it in 1579. Even before that its influence may be seen in one of the century's most ambitious compilations of didactic verse: the *First Solitary* or *Discourse on the Muses and the Poetic Frenzy*, and the *Second Solitary* or *Discourse on Music*, published at Lyons by Pontus de Tyard in 1552. This is a kind of encyclopedia, rather cryptically arranged, in which the active principle of the soul, its "daimon" or inspiration, is connected with the various branches of learning, and these in turn are related to the architecture of the universe. In Pontus de Tyard's dialogues all the arts are inextricably interwoven, music appearing as the concrete symbol of man's higher activity. This notion, constantly repeated, does indeed show that music is privileged in so far as it enables Man to express "his dim apprehension of the immeasurable resources possessed by the spiritual universe" (F. Yates). That, however, is as far as one can go.

The fact that we have come to regard sight as the intellectual sense, and the others, especially hearing, as being emotive, has given us a false perspective. No one would question the vehemence and passion that were so conspicuous in the sixteenth century; but this predominance of feeling, actual or apparent, in no way signifies that the ear had won pride of place over the eyes.

The two means of expression existed side by side and were not mutually exclusive. The lack of formal symbols in sixteenth-century literature can only mean one thing, that a large sector of psychological behavior came within the purview of painting and the representational arts. There was nothing comparable in the vocabulary and literary style of the period. The conclusion to be drawn, therefore, can and should be the other way round. The problem is to see how, in each cultural region and at each stage of development, the oral and auditive arts supplemented or counterbalanced the pictorial and plastic. By cultural region is meant principally the contrast in pace and rhythm between the countries of Northern Europe and those of the Mediterranean. The stage of development refers above all to the climacteric of 1540-1550, the decade when the most significant innovations took place. Both aspects will be briefly dealt with.

The literature of Northern Europe, still rather uncouth round about 1500, was completely transformed during the sixteenth century, partly through adopting more sophisticated methods of expressing moral concepts, but mainly as a result of developing a new-found skill in formal construction and in the devising and describing of situations that gave free rein to the imagination. Evidence of this may be seen in the belated but complete success of that elaborate analysis of architectural and sculptural motifs, the *Dream of Polyphilus,* an eccentric masterpiece of Alexandrian *ekphrasis,* which Renaissance scholarship had made fashionable. From the Pléiade down to Agrippa d'Aubigné one finds a steady development in descriptive power, accompanied by a greatly enriched style. The same applies to the England of Philip Sidney and the Elizabethans. Only the spur of imagination can account for these attempts at literary renovation, although it should be borne in mind that the Italians were far ahead of the Northerners in this flowering of poetry.

There is any amount of evidence to show how writers were striving to describe and by so doing to endow literary forms with heightened realism. This was one of the main purposes of the Pléiade; but there is no need to rely on the tedious and monumental achievements of such poets as de Baïf and Belleau. There are more unassuming examples in which enumeration and the piling on of detail give one a clear enough idea of what a graphic style could achieve. How could one better describe pottery decorated in the "naturalist" manner, so successfully employed by Palissy, than in this entry by a clerk at Blois concerning an ornamental vase? "A wide bowl like the basin of a fountain, from which delightful, outlandish monsters are scattering innumerable flowerets. It has little supports of intricate pattern, some with boldly designed landscapes, some with elephants, oxen and lions, horses, dogs and monkeys, peacocks, herons and tawny owls, vases, lamps and exploding fireworks, asps, lizards and snails, bees, butterflies and cockchafers, fairies, masks, cornucopias and other flourishes" (inventory made by F. Robertet in 1532 and recorded by L. Bonaffé). The style may strike one as being somewhat incoherent, but there is no doubting its overwhelmingly visual effect.

About the time when the descriptive faculty was gaining ground in the literature of countries which lagged behind those of the Mediterranean, Western art in general was being deflected, one might almost say permeated, by similar intellectual and moral currents. Since the Middle Ages the *storia,* or narrative with a dramatic theme, had figured prominently in painting and sculpture, and it became a major factor in the Italian Renaissance. Not only were there innovations in the setting and structure of these *storie,* but about 1540 they became increasingly complex and ambitious, developing their argument on two or three levels: cosmological (the seasons and heavenly bodies), ethical (the virtues) and historical (the family), all of them interwoven with tireless ingenuity. One has only to consider the great set-pieces, like the Francis I gallery at Fontainebleau, the Farnese cycles at Caprarola or the huge Mannerist compositions which are in effect learned treatises. The same phenomenon is apparent in the processional routes whose various stopping places were so loaded with allusive ornaments and architectural details that a guide-book was needed to explain them.

Broadly speaking, Renaissance thought has an emblematic quality resulting from the original synthesis of idea *(concetto)* and image. So incapable was it of separating the word from the likeness that there may be something to be said for ascribing to

the Renaissance a certain confusion of thought. Although the advance of civilization produced a stream of new modes and expressions, the inveterate linking of literature to the other arts involved an overall conception of man's inner nature that must be accepted at the outset. It accounts both for writers' excessively visual and statistical approach and for the way in which literature constantly impinged on the other arts. The movement was all of a piece, as is only to be expected of an age of such luxuriant, full-blooded hopes. This may well be what we really mean when we speak of the Renaissance.

Although there were plenty of attempts to discriminate between writers and artists, between the discourse and the effigy, one cannot infer that there was any real awareness of the two forms of expression being distinct. Such opposition as there was always arose from professional rivalry. Socially speaking, it is interesting to see how the intellectuals worked hand in glove, or competed against one another, for the favor not only of princes and patrons but also of the public at large. In Italy, about 1540, a memorable alliance blossomed between Aretino and Titian. The former, a man of letters who hobnobbed with artists and was practically an art critic, delivered a vehement attack on Michelangelo's *Last Judgment;* but it was prompted by *ad hoc* motives and one should not read too much into it. Artists frequently worked together—and consequently quarreled with one another—when executing royal commissions. Dorat, for instance, collaborated with Niccolò dell'Abbate and Philibert Delorme over Charles IX's state entry into Paris. Ronsard's friendship with Lescot has become legendary, and there is said to have been collusion between them in the decoration of the Louvre, where, according to Binet, "the goddess who is blowing a trumpet high up on the façade" is supposed to be advertising the *Franciade.* It was also Ronsard who from selfish motives declared war on Philibert Delorme. In a satire entitled "The Mitred Trowel" he "attacked the King for allowing preferments to be bestowed on masons and other folk of low degree." The conflict in this case was not between the champion of poetry and the great architect but between two men eager for pickings.

2

IMAGERY

"It must be admitted that the immense boon of printing, which was to increase a hundredfold man's capacity for freedom, was used at first to disseminate works that for three hundred years had been the most effective obstacles to the Renaissance" (Michelet, *The Renaissance*, Introduction XI). This is a rather crude simplification. The emergence and phenomenal output of printed works did, after all, enable the Renaissance to imbibe every kind of historical or empirical knowledge, and to display a fertility in propounding concepts only equaled by its inability to assimilate them. There was such a ferment of ideas and learning that no one could tell—or bothered to inquire—whither it was all leading. All classes shared in the process, and there emerged an entirely new phenomenon in the shape of "a great body of secular knowledge and literature, which was neither religious nor scientific nor professional and which, without being in any way hostile to religion or science, came to occupy a large area of education, letters and thought, wholly unconnected with theology and the professional disciplines" (P. O. Kristeller).

Printing also gave rise to an unprecedented demand for books and everything they stood for. This first took the form of indiscriminate collecting. There was a mania for amassing and compiling information, as is apparent not only from the works

ANDREAS VESALIUS, "DE HUMANI CORPORIS FABRICA," BASEL 1543. BIBLIOTHÈQUE NATIONALE, PARIS.

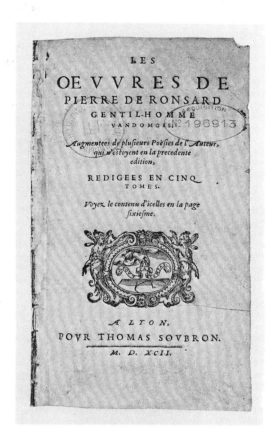

BOOK OF HOURS IN THE STYLE OF GEOFFROY TORY,
PARIS 1542. BIBLIOTHÈQUE NATIONALE, PARIS.

WORKS OF RONSARD, LYONS 1592.
BIBLIOTHÈQUE NATIONALE, PARIS.

G.B. DELLA PORTA, "DE HUMANA PHYSIOGNOMONIA,"
MILAN 1586. BIBLIOTECA AMBROSIANA, MILAN.

MICHELE MERCATI, "METALLOTHECA IN VATICANO," 1589.
BIBLIOTHÈQUE NATIONALE, PARIS.

of Rabelais and later Montaigne, but also, in a different sphere, from those of Paracelsus. This bookish accumulation of facts was reflected in the arts. The hoards of bright cultural nuggets may have resulted finally in the minting of new ideas; but since at the outset they were not in any way classified, they involved a general confusion of functions. The physician would use the language of rhetoric, and the ordinary story-teller would take whole passages from Virgil or Plutarch, not hesitating to parody or plagiarize them. Ovid or Vitruvius, Seneca or Boethius might well be harnessed to a work on politics or the theory of music. The Renaissance was the age of undifferentiated culture, as opposed on the one hand to the rigidly compartmental and classified culture which had been the glory of the Middle Ages, and on the other to the culture organized from within by reason which was to be characteristic of the classical era. The old hierarchical system had been swept away by the desire for reading and encyclopedic knowledge; the principles of the new system based on logic had not yet been worked out. There was an omnivorous appetite for facts, but nowhere does there seem to have been any grasp of the unifying methods that would make for regular coordination and coherence. Philosophers were slow to inquire into such methods. When, finally, Bacon did so in his *Novum Organum*, he rejected a great mass of the factual archives which made up the "science" of the sixteenth century.

In the main "questions of principle were ignored. The old theoretical categories and cosmologies were nearly always accepted uncritically, apart from complications resulting from a better acquaintance with the texts on which they were based. The stock of knowledge was enormously enriched, so that abstract laws gave way to perceptual 'models', sometimes inspired by genius, such as the Copernican system or the first allusions to the circulation of the blood" (R. Klein and A. Chastel, 1964). It seemed as if every human activity could be defined and imparted. Treatises were written, not merely on ethics or natural science, but on cooking, siege warfare and riding. There was an insatiable curiosity about practical problems, which meant that scholarship as well as observation must be tabulated. At the same time, however, in the realm of metaphysics men were seeking a kind of "learning without concepts, expressed wholly by means of images."

One of the most familiar results of the sixteenth century's thirst for facts was the marvelous proliferation of descriptive knowledge, made possible by books and, above all, by illustrations, which became the most powerful instrument for diffusing information. There is no need to dwell on so obvious a point. Scholars have reckoned (heaven knows on what basis) that by 1547, after less than a century of existence, printing had put into circulation over twenty-two million books. An important part, in some cases an essential part, of this vast output consisted of illustrative plates. The middle years of the century produced monumental books in every field: in 1543, Vesalius' *Fabrica*; in 1544, Sebastian Münster's *Cosmography*; the synopses of the naturalists Konrad Gesner and Pierre Belon, to be followed by the huge compendium of Giambattista Della Porta; in architecture, the treatises of Serlio (from 1540 on) and Jean Martin's French translation of Vitruvius in 1547. There were many works on archaeology by the Humanists.

This outpouring was only natural for men who were constantly brought up against the "exotic" remoteness of distant lands and the "historical" remoteness of antiquity, and who had a marked tendency to regard the latter as being of greater moment. The big publishing houses usually opened their books, whether works of erudition or poetry, with a portentous frontispiece, like a fanfare of trumpets. Its elaborate design and architectural trimmings provided a worthy accompaniment to a book's intellectual power and were displayed with a disarming gusto never to be recaptured. In the work of that eager student of typography Geoffroy Tory, the title page, despite its rich architectonic layout, retains a certain simplicity. In the second half of the century the complex devices of the title page are intended as an intimation of the contents and scope of the book. The extraordinary frontispieces to the treatises of Mercati and Stoer are veritable picture-preludes, brilliantly evoking the book's program through symbols. In the imagery it made use of, printing found a powerful ally.

CERCEAU,
VETERIS,"
PAGE 24).
RBE, HAMBURG.

SEPTEM PLANETÆ

Septē
Hominis
ætatibus respondentes scilicet
1. INFANTIÆ
2. PVERITIÆ
3. ADOLESCENTIÆ
4. IVVENTVTI
5. VIRILI ÆTATI
6. SENILI ÆTATI
7. SENECTÆ DECREPITÆ
Cum eorundem in easdem operationibus
et effectibus elegatissimis figuris
depicti
Homo natus de muliere breui viuens tem:
pore repletur multis miserys
Job. 14
Dies annorum nostrorum in ipsis
SEPTVAGINTA āni erunt
psal. 89
Gerardus de Jode excu.
anno. 1581.
Mar. de vos iuen.

FRONTISPIECE OF "SEPTEM PLANETAE," 1581, DESIGNED BY GERARD DE JODE AND MARTIN DE VOS.
BIBLIOTHÈQUE NATIONALE, PARIS.

42

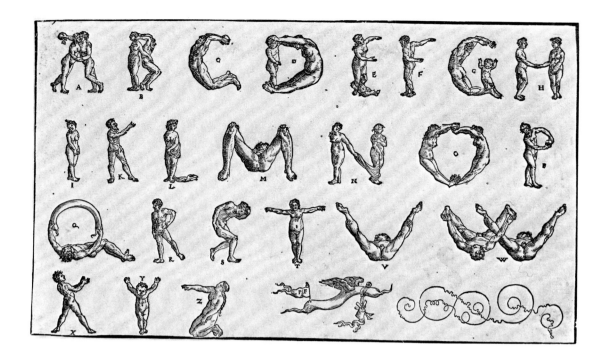

PETER FLETTNER
(OR FLÖTNER, ACTIVE 1523-1546).
ANTHROPOMORPHIC ALPHABET.
ABOUT 1534.
WOODCUT. ALBERTINA, VIENNA.

UNUSED DESIGN FOR THE FRONTISPIECE OF LORENZ STOER, "GEOMETRIA ET PERSPECTIVA,"
AUGSBURG 1567. INK DRAWING. STAATLICHE GRAPHISCHE SAMMLUNG, MUNICH.

JACQUES ANDROUET DU
"FRAGMENTA STRUCTURAE
ORLÉANS 1550 (PLATE ON
MUSEUM FÜR KUNST UND GEW

41

ENGINEER AND PHILOSOPHER
THE ART OF RECOLLECTION

Two remarkable men illustrate for us the type of ratiocination in which imaginative power counted for far more than the ability to formulate concepts. The eccentric engineer, Jerome Cardan (Geronimo Cardano), and the heroic philosopher, Giordano Bruno, possessed a massive genius of almost unlimited range and versatility. The bewildering maelstrom of their careers may be said to reflect the variety and truly international character of their abilities and inquiries.

Cardan, the engineer, inventor and physician, encountered so many vicissitudes and conflicts that he was impelled, like Cellini, to write a book vindicating himself. It begins with a character sketch, based on his "nativity," which is so inconsequent as to be practically incredible: "clever, honest, ethical, sensual, cheerful, devout, loyal, inquisitive, inventive, specious, cunning, caustic... envious, pathetic, treacherous, a wizard and a spellbinder, ill-starred, a lickspittle and a lecher... my temperament and character are so full of contradictions that even my closest friends do not know me" (*Liber de exemplis C. geniturarum,* translated by J. Dayre). It is unlikely that Cardan was taken in by his own volatility and the exuberance of his ego; but one may point out that he was using psychological terms as an unwonted and rather provocative means of interpreting the general aptitudes of man as the qualities of a single individual. It is a case of Pico della Mirandola's metaphysical eulogy of the universal man being debased into an unwarranted condensation of one hypertrophied personality.

However keen the critic's eye, in Cardan the scientist and the wizard are inseparable, for both are facets of the same quality. At the age of four he awoke to behold an enchanting vision: "I saw many images like ethereal bodies made up of tiny rings...

They floated slowly upwards, wheeling and falling on my left... There were citadels, houses, horses and riders, grassy spaces, weapons, instruments of music... trumpeters whose call I seemed to hear" (*De vita propria liber,* translated by J. Dayre). Cardan always examined his dreams, which to him were revelations, and expounded them in his biography as the fabric of his life. Nor was he alone in being thus preoccupied with what he had dreamed. He had a natural predilection for creating clear, potent, three-dimensional images of the kind known to modern psychology as "eidetic." They threw him into fits of ecstasy or panic, filling his narrative with irrational fears and premonitions. Here may be found the origin of a complete psychic demonology. "One day at Pavia I happened to glance at my hands, and at the base of my right ring-finger I saw a sword the color of blood." This he interpreted as a threat to his son, with further implications besides. Cardan, moreover, was wholly typical of his age. One has only to think of Ronsard fighting with drawn sword against the spirits of darkness.

The men of the sixteenth century, unlike their "Gothic-minded" predecessors, recognized and confronted these diabolical forces quite openly. It would seem as if all mental restraints on their flights of fancy had been swept away. On the other hand, the sixteenth century, unlike the age that followed it, did not see any contradiction between its fantasies and the dictates of reason. Intellect and imagination did not conflict. No doubt the advance of rationalism made men more sceptical. Astrology fell under a cloud. Wizards were mistrusted and sometimes denounced, but more because of their behavior than as a matter of principle. The vehemence and personal nature of the attacks on them show how seriously they were taken. Everyday language was extraordinarily emphatic in this respect, alluding constantly to tutelary gods or "ascendants." Fables as such were no longer believed, but there was much talk of the forces they symbolized, such as the dark, disturbing mysteries of nature.

All that was new, telling, big with consequences, was looked upon as wondrous. In his autobiography Cardan numbers among the "prodigies of nature," indeed as the first and rarest of all, "the fact that I was born in this century when the whole world has been discovered, whereas the ancients knew scarcely more than a third of it" (*De vita propria liber,* ch. XLVI, translated by J. Dayre). Cardan's faculty of enthusiasm was boundless, and it enabled him to share in the new vision of space, in that "silent revolution working at the heart of the sixteenth century" (A. Dupront) which had been engendered by the exploration of the world, the circling of the globe, the realization of the earth's true extent.

Cardan devotes the same care to relating his amazing misfortunes and blessings, his successes as a skillful engineer and his obsession with the bizarre. The turbid stream of his thought is shot through with striking and even lofty observations, the more vivid because of the ingenuousness with which they are expressed. In describing the prerogatives *(proprietates)* that have stood him in good stead, among which he reckons his premonitions and the vicissitudes of his destiny, Cardan finds it quite natural to point to the gift of "splendor," which, he says, "I succeeded in gradually increasing." Splendor, which of course he does not define, seems to be a sort of inner radiance, the buoyant happiness that comes from mental activity. "Fulfilment and splendor—these I obtained partly with the help of my genius, partly by exercising it. The art of writing and of improvising lessons I owe entirely to my familiar spirit *(genius)* and to splendor." The sixteenth century is full of such references to the divine afflatus and to the frenzy and violence of genius. It was in the striving after genius that temperament and achievement were united. It may be seen in Cardan's cloudy reflections and the portentous prophecies of Paracelsus; in Ronsard's noble verse, in the writings of Michelangelo's devoted admirers, in the pathetic life of Tasso. All are imbued with that grandeur and vigor which for us constitute one of the finest and most flamboyant "commonplaces" of the age.

The same characteristics reappear in Giordano Bruno, whose stormy, indomitable life reveals all the hazards, indiscretions and hectic impulses that beset a great empiricist. His spiritual pilgrimage led him, by way of the dogmatic Averroism of Padua, through Calvin's Geneva, swiftly rejected, to the Paris of Henry III, England, Wittenberg and Frankfurt. He went to the stake in February 1600, a martyr not to any doctrine, still less to the "new" learning, but to the ideal of an independent mind. Far superior to Cardan in education and style, Bruno was convinced that he had within his grasp the cardinal proofs of the Spirit, of which the greatest was love. There could be no knowledge of the soul without a philosophy of love, no philosophy without a cosmology. In one sense he followed Plotinus and Nicholas of Cusa—or Marsilio Ficino; in another, he was a disciple of Lucretius and Copernicus. He set out as a Peripatetic and ended as a Neo-Platonist. The Aristotelian concepts of matter and form were deprived by Bruno of their rational discreteness, the former comprising inert fact, the latter synthetic principle, so that they became twin facets of the universal soul; and this, being inexhaustibly dynamic, existed sometimes within and sometimes apart from the divine power.

Can such a philosophy be described as "pantheism"? The most recent historians prefer to emphasize the sixteenth century's inveterate though confused desire for synthesis, which in this case can be seen, so to speak, in every dimension (P. O. Kristeller, P. H. Michel). Speculation gravitated towards the compelling, even obsessive concept of the soul in a state of constant anguish and deprivation. Not only was this admirably suited to the hypersensitivity of the Renaissance, but owing to the perpetual oscillation between one plane and the other, the simultaneous acceptance of categories that were later to be more carefully distinguished, there grew up a thoroughly anti-Cartesian outlook, intuitive and "emblematic," which inspired such astonishing works as the *Eroici furores*. One may ask whether this heroic ardor, this spiritual frenzy which alone made life worth living, was indeed divine love, at once sensual and intellectual. At all events, it was embodied in the sixteenth century by verse as inspired as that, later on, of the English metaphysical poets and dictated, likewise, by images of almost unparalleled vehemence and dread.

Such were the forces that aroused, and tended to unify, Renaissance man's immense lust for knowledge. Thanks to the scope and vigor of his mind, Bruno was able to embrace, for the last time, the vital themes of Neo-Platonism and combine them with the facts of the new cosmology, these facts themselves being interpreted in accordance with the language of mythography. He mastered practically all the knowledge of his time and fitted it into a world-view, rational and supra-rational, in which the chain of being alternately narrows and widens in unbroken succession. For his view, at every point, shows an awareness of the underlying relations of all beings, both in the form and in the spirit. In this, Bruno fulfilled a deep and long-standing aspiration of the period. His activity thus ties up with another aspect, long neglected but recently brought to light, of the encyclopedic bent of the sixteenth century. The men of the Renaissance made up for their lack of logical, systematic categories by adopting certain mental processes inherited from the Schoolmen. Perfected and instilled by teachers with a view to stimulating the imaginative faculty, these methods consisted of the *artificiosa memoria*. It was hoped that they could be made more flexible and efficient than university instruction. Their principle was familiar, for it had been set out by Cicero in the *De oratore* and popularized by medieval writers. It consisted in using the retentive powers of the mind, based on the conjunction of spatial selection *(loci)* and visual points of reference *(imagines)*, in such a way as to generate instantaneous manifold associations. It was a rhetorical device that lent itself readily to general use. Quintilian had suggested that speeches should be prepared by setting out the various points in a hypothetical design resembling, for instance, the structure of a building. Each component, both outside and in, such as doors, windows and cornices, would thus be "motivated." Once the whole outline had been sketched, it would only remain to recapitulate the complex image in terms of this spatial pattern. The method was clearly far more graphic and picturesque than the "Barocco, Baralipton" and other *memoria technica* of Scholasticism (F. Yates, 1966).

In this way spatial description acquired organic validity, wholly distinct from that of logical deduction, but deriving a certain effectiveness from the vigor it imparted to the argument. Giordano Bruno followed the example of many others in advocating the fullest use of visual images, whereby the Renaissance imitated and perfected a favorite practice of the Schoolmen. A number of writers were persuaded that the methods of Antiquity were well worth adopting and that the visualizing technique should be carried still further. They felt that more methodical arrangement might ultimately provide a sort of universal repository of thought. This was attempted by one Giulio Camillo of Udine, who died in 1544. He taught at Bologna and later had some success as professor of *ars memorativa*, first at Milan and then in France in the service of Francis I.

His book *Idea del Teatro*, published at Florence in 1550, describes a curious model, which had in fact been exhibited at the French court. It consisted of a wooden mock-up in which rows of drawers were set above one another in an amphitheater, exhaustively labelled and indexed. They were so designed that planetary deities and mythological figures rose up in corresponding tiers, in which the various orders, cosmic and psychological, supernatural and moral, echoed one another from top to bottom. In the center a pyramid with God at its apex stood for "the respiration of all things" and reminded the beholder that the Christian cosmogony could be superimposed on the universal framework.

One can see why, apart from its practical utility, this contraption was well received; for it brought together, as it were, all the matrices, by combining the compartmented tiers of the classical amphitheater with the concentric rings of the Christian paradise. Camillo, however, seems to have been aiming at something more than a working model, namely "a demonstration of universal truth." His influence on philosophy and cosmology must have been considerable, and he may even have contemplated some reform. The very idea of giving the forces of the universe symbolic reality and thereby making them wholly comprehensible, this in itself tended to change Man by strengthening his powers of synthesis (R. Bernheimer, 1950). One can sense that the men who pursued such inquiries usually had some utopian proclivity at the back of their minds. There are concrete applications of this typically Renaissance outlook that will repay investigation when we come to consider cities and the projects of town-planners.

RENAISSANCE AND REFORMATION

Unde paganismus iste in Christianitate? Aut unde mundanus iste
Christus non de caelo loquens sed de terra?

ERASMUS, *Paraphrase in Psalm*, 1

Any gradualist interpretation of the sixteenth century is ruled out by the mere fact of the anti-Roman Reformers' sudden emergence and the overwhelming response they evoked in northern Europe. The "crisis of the Renaissance" is made instantly apparent by the immense religious drama in which the anti-Papist and Roman protagonists combined horrible ferocity with a heartfelt renewal of Christian piety. The entire century reverberated to the conflict, even though the issues it involved did not always appear in the same light, either to monarchs or to thinkers. Different motives may have actuated Henry VIII in creating the autocephalous Anglican church, Calvin in setting up his Puritan republic at Geneva, and the humble Huguenot neophyte who smashed the stained glass in his parish church. The fact remains that men of all classes and walks of life, representing commons, clergy and nobility alike, found themselves sooner or later on one side or the other and were compelled willy-nilly to make their choice.

Passions were fearfully intensified, for there is an inveterate tendency in crises of this kind whereby the urge to freedom of those who have rebelled swiftly begets authoritarian institutions which become oppressive in their turn. Such was the case in Geneva, Saxony and England. The challenge to orthodoxy and authority, moreover, led the Church itself to modify many points of doctrine and practice. The proliferation of new orders and the appearance of "reformist" and "mystical" movements within the church were no less remarkable a consequence of the Reformation than was the Council of Trent, with its attempt to redefine the foundations of Christian practice and belief. Catholicism felt the need to reform itself from within, just as much as to combat heresy with dungeons and the stake.

Among its many aspects the Reformation comprised both a longing for a purer Christian life and a terrible propensity to violence. These deserve careful analysis, for among the most significant and unexpected features of the crisis was a formidable wave of "iconoclasm." The Renaissance provided the last occasion when Christendom was rent by schism over the question of images.

Erasmus profoundly distrusted what were known as the "works" of religion—services and ritual devotions—for he avowedly regarded them as superstitions from which the Christian faith ought to be delivered. The innumerable ways, popular or patrician, in which saints were worshipped and relics venerated, affronted his sense of Christian dignity. In this respect he was at one with the Reformers (and even anticipated them), for like them he rejected the pagan idolatry underlying many practices that upheld the authority of the Mendicant Orders and lined the pockets of St Peter. Although his *Modus Orandi Deum* was written in 1524 to combat Lutheran intransigence and vindicate, as the Fathers of the Church had done, a lawful use of images, it nonetheless contained, like his early pamphlets, many scathing passages against "Gothic" demonstrations of piety and monkish mumbo-jumbo. "At Canterbury he saw the devout kissing the shoes of St Thomas Becket... He thought such foolery should only be tolerated until it could be forbidden without causing a riot" (A. Renaudet). Those who were honored in the name of the Virgin or of Christ or of St Paul were no more than debauched rakes and lecherous whores, *Lasciva meretricula... tumulentum quemdam nebulonem.*

With the unerring perception for which he is celebrated the great humanist of Rotterdam reiterated his disgust at the frivolity of subjects beloved of ecclesiastical artists, such as the nakedness of Bathsheba. He criticized not merely the "Gothic" practices of northern Europe but also the morals of Italians, which were already being affected by the Renaissance. "In Italy I saw a Carthusian monastery near Pavia. The church was entirely covered, inside and out, with white marble. Almost everything in it—altars, pillars, tombs—was of marble. Why waste all that money in order that a handful of monks should sing Mass in a marble church that is more of a burden than an asset to them, for it is constantly filled with visitors who come merely to gape at the marble?" (*Colloquia, convivium religiosum*, Opera, ed. Leyden, 1, 685).

Erasmus' waspish complaint drew an ironical rejoinder from Burckhardt: "He takes the sumptuous tomb of Thomas Becket and the costly marbles of the Charterhouse at Pavia as the text for a mawkish sermon on charity. The money should have been given to the poor; flowers would have provided sufficient adornment for a saint's tomb. No doubt; but the poor would soon have spent the money and we should not have the Charterhouse at Pavia." There is something to be said for this view. Erasmus' sardonic remark shows how genuine spiritual feeling came to erect a defensive barrier against the new trends, which it regarded with the same distrust as the old superstitions. Before long the Reformation, that German and ultimately European avatar of the human and religious *renovatio*, so long foretold and so eagerly awaited but never yet realized, would combine with an anti-southern reaction to imperil the concord that was just beginning to emerge between the new culture and Christian philosophy.

The conflict between paganism and Christianity flared up once more and the feeling of revulsion at the childish corruption of much religious life was by no means confined to the North. One has only to read the diatribe of Charles V's imperial secretary, Alfonso de Valdés, itself a product of Humanism but also dictated by tragic circumstance: "Do you ask for another sign of paganism?... We have assigned to our saints all the functions that were carried out by heathen gods. Mars has been replaced by St James, and St George, Neptune by St Elmo, Bacchus by St Martin, Aeolus by St Barbara, Venus by Mary Magdalene. As for Aesculapius, we have divided his duties up among a number of saints:

for ordinary diseases, St Cosmas and St Damian; for epidemics, St Roch; for the eyes, St Lucy; for the teeth, St Apollinus. Then we have St Agatha for cats, St Anthony and St Eligius for other animals, St Simon and St Jude for false witness, St Blaise for sneezing. I know not what purpose these inventions and dispensations serve, if it be not that of making us appear wholly pagan and taking away from Jesus Christ the love we owe to him alone" (*Dialogue concerning the Events at Rome*, published after 1527). Such bitterness resembles the sternest denunciations of Calvin.

Men like this great master of prose and logic, or the mighty thinker Melanchthon, gave utterance to the longing to "dematerialize" not merely church services but all spiritual exercises by resorting to Holy Writ and music. The idea had been propounded by Luther, and the Germans found in it a plain statement of faith that was to transform them for many years to come. True religion could only accommodate simple rites, such as choral singing, that were innocent of any physical appeal. All other observances suddenly became anathema, and the innumerable preachers of Augsburg, Geneva, Scotland and the Ile-de-France fulminated endlessly against the "idolatry" of those who built churches and carved statues of the Virgin and saints. The hallmark of such radicals, their first demonstration of freedom consisted usually in a "massacre" of images. These ravages were carried out on a formidable scale. Moral exaltation, as so often happens, was accompanied by an element of hysteria and needless brutality, resulting in an orgy of desecration. The Dutch chronicler Van Mander (1604) gives an indignant account of the altarpieces destroyed or damaged by the Huguenots; he notes that the *Crucifixion* in the church of Saint-Jacques at Bruges was spared "for the sake of its artistic merit" (in fact the painting was preserved by being given a black coating, on which the Ten Commandments were written in gold).

It was above all French art that suffered, owing to the barbarity of the civil conflict. According to a Venetian ambassador, "The Reformers have destroyed so many churches and other sacred buildings that a decade of Crown revenues would not suffice to rebuild them" (*Reports*, II, 133). The Huguenots' enemies denounced and harried them ferociously, but they did not exaggerate their misdeeds: the treasury of Saint-Denis pillaged, the desecration of the cathedrals at Rouen, Orléans, Bourges, Jumièges, la Charité-sur-Loire, Saint-Etienne de Périgueux... hundreds of Romanesque churches in flames, statues smashed, illuminated manuscripts burned, precious objects defiled or melted down. It was mainly in the provinces, between 1559 and 1569, that the worst excesses were committed—excesses which repression and massacre served only to exacerbate. In 1566 Caron painted a strange vision of France in the guise of the horrors perpetrated at Rome by the Triumvirs. An indifferent picture in the Gadagne Museum at Lyons records the sack of the town by armed bands led by the Baron des Adrets, the burning of works of art in the cathedral square and the demolition of fifty statues from the façade. In 1572 the Massacre of St Bartholomew was preceded and followed by a paroxysm of desecration. As Etienne Pasquier sadly noted, "Whenever the Huguenot is master, he destroys images, shatters tombs and loots the oblations of churches."

This breach between the Biblical text, revered as the word of God, and the sacred image, repudiated with a vengeance, went far beyond a mere aesthetic conflict. It led to a fundamental disruption arising from the fact that art, which intellectuals like Erasmus did not take very seriously or regard as a significant factor, was also belittled in the minds of ordinary people as making no contribution to human dignity. This goes far to explain the conflicting attitudes of general opinion, for there was an instinctive reaction in the opposite sense. It was not only poets like Ronsard who leaped to the defence of statues and pictures. There is clear evidence of a deep-rooted antagonism between books and images, between one culture expressed in writing and another displayed in form and color; an antagonism that was never so marked in European civilization as during the Renaissance. To this internal "polarization" one must add the nascent hostility between the attitudes of northern and southern Europe, and finally, the religious schism itself. The concatenation of all these factors led to fanaticism on either side. Wherever they clashed one finds turmoil, the "crisis of the Renaissance."

We have already quoted Jakob Burckhardt, who had no liking for the narrow fanaticism of the sixteenth century and therefore emphasized with some irony the awkward position of the arts in northern Europe, where, he felt, the new culture of the South had never been more than skin-deep. Some northerners, of course, such as Dürer and his friend Pirckheimer, or Cranach and the Elector of Saxony, were genuinely inspired by it; but in the main, according to Burckhardt, it did not amount to much more than "a certain vanity" in wanting to have oneself painted by a master. This is rather unfair to various other enlightened circles such as that of the Vienna humanist Conrad Celtis and that of the publishers of Basel. On the whole, however, it is true that "German humanism tended to be hostile to art or, like the philosophers of antiquity, was fundamentally alien to it." The most serious and imminent rift, therefore, lay in the issue whether there was any point in projecting ideas and concepts in visible form. This new-born controversy was the main theme of the sixteenth century, for it went far beyond a purely religious context. For some the purifying of Christian thought mattered far more than any concession to aesthetics; others considered the danger of paganizing tendencies far less serious than the loss of visual representation.

It was between these two poles that the "crisis of the Renaissance" developed its maximum tension. Only after a generation of conflict, which was not, however, universal, and which set fairly well defined limits to the reformed religion, did the latter principle triumph. As a counterpart to iconoclasm there occurred a general paganizing of artistic idiom, whether sacred or secular, which neither the Reformation nor the Counter-Reformation could undo, accompanied throughout the century by a transformation of religious imagery whose significance has sometimes been overlooked. Implicit in that transformation is the whole new world of forms which Renaissance art brought into existence, and which range far beyond the cautious or critical postures of Humanism. The latter had never evolved a body of doctrine that could either replace or be wholly assimilated to the trends of Christian thought. The historical approach of the new school of clerks, Erasmus and the rest, postulated the hope of an ideal unity, even of a universal religion. The same hope was long cherished by those who may be called the Christian Cabbalists, from Reuchlin to Postel, whose recondite metaphysics were based on hidden affinities between Biblical philology and Hebrew esoterism.

This movement had some success, but was largely a matter of preaching to the converted. It was only the verbal and pictorial forms of the new culture that continued to gush forth in full spate. The countries that had retained their fondness for images readily adopted the new modes in sacred and secular art. One need only mention the example of France, where so many façades and doorways were decorated with medallions of "heroes" and "tempietti," which themselves advertised the merits of the new style. The Pléiade poets, following their Italian mentors, fully realized that they must keep abreast of the times, and that poetry could only be renewed by resorting to classical fable and the grand manner. For the men of 1530 or 1550 the one means of giving sculpture and architecture their full value was by exploiting the resources of antiquity and matching the masterpieces of Rome. How could religious art stand aloof? Neither Raphael nor Michelangelo dreamed of doing so, and their example led to a torrent of "paganism" which engulfed the Church both before and after the time when Erasmus in the North and Valdés in the South had so nobly protested against the danger of idolatry. The sanctuary became a classical temple, and Christ assumed the guise of Apollo. Innumerable liberties accompanied the celebrated works of genius that modernized and thereby protected the traditional emblems of Christendom.

The Erasmians' uneasy tolerance of images shows that they did not appreciate the full extent of the problem—nor, for that matter, did the churchmen assembled at the Council of Trent. It is astonishing to see that, just when the iconoclasts in the North were waging a ruthless campaign against the chaste Madonnas and Saints of the churches in the Loire valley and eastern France, elsewhere there was a vogue for religious paintings as seemingly frivolous and worldly as those of Parmigianino. In the occasionally disingenuous Pietàs or Madonnas and in the epicene Christs by Rosso or Antoine Caron there is no mistaking the profane character of the beauty with which the artist is serving the Church. There

was a taste for pomp, a mania for huge, spectacular cycles, to which we shall return in due course. After all, the completion of St Peter's at Rome, so fiercely contested by the Reformers, remained throughout the century an ambition tenaciously pursued by the Papacy and by all Catholics.

The fact that the Reformers' piety found an outlet in the inverted superstition of iconoclasm makes all the more striking the contrary reaction on the part of the Catholics who rallied to protect the holy images used in the Mass, and especially in the worship of the Virgin. This reaction was not merely an occasion for windy rhetoric; it sometimes brought to fruition sublime feelings whose grandeur may be seen in the Spanish mystics. Here one must recall the manner in which the visions of St Teresa of Avila combined the benison of religious ecstasy with the most outspoken eroticism: "This anguish," she wrote, "was not physical but spiritual, although the body partook of it." One of the assets of Protestantism was that it fulfilled the desire for a new "image-hating" education, which was provided by the formidable Melanchthon and by such universities as Strasbourg and Geneva, reinforced by a stream of publications. Meanwhile the founder of the Jesuits, taking inspiration from similar sources and fully alive to the unprecedented character of the age, followed a different analytical path in his efforts to adjust a reinvigorated Christianity to an inevitable national and cultural diversity. The pedagogy of Ignatius's *Spiritual Exercises* was based on the compulsive power of images, and it resulted in a further evolution, indeed an activation, of Christian iconography, which varied in its nature and effects according to time and circumstance. But, in accordance with the contemporary garrulousness and love of complexity, it led to an increasing intricacy of themes which was intended to enrich the doctrinal aspect of painting. This trend ran contrary to the call for evangelic simplicity which some churchmen of the Council of Trent, under the impact of the Reformation, had re-echoed in the name of the Church of Rome.

THE REACTION OF IMAGES

One of the most naïve exponents of the new, overloaded imagery was Vasari, whose altarpiece of the Immaculate Conception *(1535) used a jumble of* concetti *to produce what he regarded as a masterpiece of theological learning. His pretensions were the more absurd since it was he who, writing as a critic, admonished his compatriot Pontormo for the obscurity of his work in the choir of San Lorenzo in Florence, which he had been commissioned to decorate in 1548. The foreground was filled by Christ in glory, seated between a Resurrection and a Flood, which were executed with such boisterousness that they evoked cries of protest and the work was painted over in the seventeenth century. In 1568 Vasari observed that no one could make head or tail of "this Christ on high resurrecting the dead, with God the Father at His feet creating Adam and Eve." The painting may not really have been so difficult to interpret, but the fact remains that Pontormo, a man of unbalanced and hectic temper, had used a sort of iconographic shorthand in order to extol the idea of redemption through grace (Charles de Tolnay), and a style which consisted wholly in the lavish display of nude figures. One is aware of a double allusion to Michelangelo underlying this controversy. Vasari envied Pontormo his consummate pastiche of the style of the* Last Judgment; *and had he known more about religious feeling he might well have detected in the unwonted portrayal of Christ triumphant another echo of Michelangelo's manner, this time in a doctrinal sense.*

The case of Michelangelo emphasizes the direction in which the Catholic Reform was moving and enables one to identify the dogmatic, authoritarian tendencies of the Council of Trent. Between 1530 and 1550 a number of distinguished men, aware how critical the situation was, forgathered in the salon of Vittoria Colonna, where Michelangelo had an honored place. They, too, aimed at a richer spiritual life, to be attained through grace and justification by faith based on a livelier consciousness of an immediate relationship with Christ crucified. Not only did these men acknowledge unreservedly the orthodox Catholic creed, but the reform they desired was to be accomplished within the context of art and not by denying it. Among the most splendid manifestoes of their outlook was the great "Psalm of Penitence" of Michelangelo's Last Judgment *(1535-1541). It is clear from the aesthetic* and theological assessment of this work by Aretino and Doni that they were impressed not only by Michelangelo's new freedom of style, in which space no longer had any reality, but by his daring use of concetti. Such a painting alone was enough to expose the futility of iconoclasm. It displayed figures in the nude, kindled the sensual imagination and clothed divinity in human flesh; it contained everything that the Reformation rejected, and withal it skillfully expounded a doctrinal lesson whose significance could not be ignored. Thus the mannered and rather stilted iconography of painters like Vasari did not exclude this further development, bound up with mystical renewal of the Catholic faith and giving rise to a purely personal interpretation of a new spiritual message.

On a very different plane this was also to be the objective of El Greco, when from Venetian Mannerism in the use of color he evolved a highly original and dramatic treatment. Towards the end of the century one finds many similar examples of attempts to reconcile art and religion. Artists with unprecedented breadth of vision were, it seems, determined to prove that pictures could be made to fulfil the needs of the inner life.

El Greco's Burial of Count Orgaz is the obvious exemplar of this school. But there is a noteworthy instance of a comparable synthesis of Tridentine evangelism and the individual grand manner in one of the masterpieces of Venetian painting: Tintoretto's vast picture cycle in the Scuola di San Rocco (about 1580). The robust treatment and a rather light-hearted indifference to accuracy and polish are typical of the Venetians, who ignored the frigid mannerism then in fashion and remained steadfastly attached to pomp and lavishness. Yet Tintoretto's cycle fulfils a didactic purpose. In defiance of tradition it says nothing about the life of the Brotherhood's patron saint, but uses an ingenious selection of scenes from the Old and New Testaments to illustrate the theme of the Eucharist. The great hall where Tintoretto exhibited his powers to the full, as Michelangelo had done in the Sistine Chapel, is in fact the oratory of the Scuola. These paintings do in a sense reassemble the elements of Christian iconography around the central truth of the Mass; for both by design and in the freedom of its inspiration the San Rocco cycle is intentionally directed against heresy (R. Hüttinger, 1963). It gives a conclusive answer to the great controversy of the sixteenth century.

JEAN DE GOURMONT (ACTIVE 1483-1551). THE NATIVITY, ABOUT 1522-1526.
FROM THE CHAPEL OF THE CHÂTEAU D'ECOUEN. LOUVRE, PARIS.

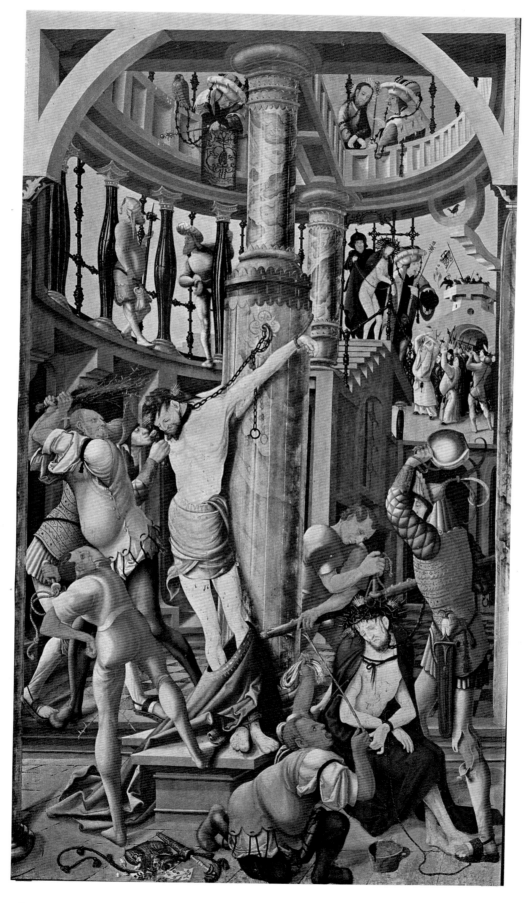

JÖRG RATGEB (ABOUT 1480-1526). THE SCOURGING OF CHRIST, 1519. INNER LEFT WING OF THE HERRENBERG ALTARPIECE.
STAATSGALERIE, STUTTGART.

JAN VAN HEMESSEN (ABOUT 1500-1566). ST JEROME IN THE DESERT, 1531. MUSEU NACIONAL DE ARTE ANTIGA, LISBON.

JACOPO PONTORMO (1494-1557). ST JEROME, ABOUT 1525-1530. NIEDERSÄCHSISCHE GALERIE, HANOVER.

RAFFAELLO DEL COLLE (ABOUT 1490-1566). MADONNA AND CHILD WITH THE YOUNG ST JOHN. UNDATED.
THE WALTERS ART GALLERY, BALTIMORE.

EL GRECO (1541-1614). PIETÀ, ABOUT 1580-1585.
S. S. NIARCHOS COLLECTION.

TINTORETTO (1518-1594). THE NATIVITY, ABOUT 1580.
SCUOLA GRANDE DI SAN ROCCO, VENICE.

ANTOINE CARON (1521-1599). THE RESURRECTION, ABOUT 1589. MUSÉE DÉPARTEMENTAL DE L'OISE, BEAUVAIS.

II

UNITY
OF THE DIVIDED WEST

NORTH AND SOUTH

Some say that in Flanders the painting of trees and clothes is unsurpassed; and there are those who credit the Italians with greater skill in portraying the nude and representing symmetry or proportions.

FRANCISCO DE HOLLANDA, *Dialogues on Painting*, III

During the sixteenth century the development of language and art in European countries ran along similar lines, in so far as they were equally affected by a single, strongly marked cultural trend. There was widespread adoption of a more scholarly Latin and a Roman style of sculpture, together with idioms, historical allusions and a rhetorical manner, all bearing a classical, Mediterranean stamp. The extent and significance of this trend, however, varied considerably from place to place.

Although by 1530 Paris, Nuremberg and Cracow had their avowed humanist devotees of the arts, they did not, as we have seen, represent more than a tributary of the main stream. Writing and thought were being stimulated by new literary modes (however monotonous and artificial some of them may seem), lapidary inscriptions, odes and declamatory epistles. In Hungary and Poland, in the Netherlands, France and Spain, and lastly in England, the reform of everyday speech and literature, of the vernacular as it was called, represented a paradoxical but important consequence of the diffusion of Humanism and Italian literature. "Humanism nourished and ripened that element in national cultures which was to enable them one day not to forget but to transcend it." In the countries of Western Europe, with the Pléiade and Spenser and the Spanish lyrics, great poetic ambitions flowered in the rays of the Southern sun.

It is clear that the same process was taking place in the arts. Gothic architecture was no longer esteemed—"Gothic," that is, in the depreciatory connotation applied by Southerners to the products of the North. It was still practised, with stale persistence, in Brussels, Cologne and Prague, but in Portugal, Spain and France the spirit of renewal very early gave it a decorative inflection which prepared the way for the introduction of minor but picturesque forms from the South. New features, such as chapels, baptismal fonts and tombs were inserted among the old, whose style was gradually effaced by them. This slow transformation, admirably illustrated by a fine example like the church of Saint-Eustache at Paris, gives further evidence of the stylistic tension caused by the fusion of antithetical traditions.

It was not long before French master-masons or, as they were beginning to be called, "architectors," declared their independence. This occurred unmistakably in the reign of Henry II. Lescot and Philibert Delorme who had been followers of the Italian school, decided to strike out on their own, except in so far as Italy could provide assistance in the form of classical prototypes; and even these were being copied and engraved by Frenchmen like Dupérac, working at Rome, who claimed to equal if not excel the Italians in their research and publications. In 1559 Androuet Du Cerceau dedicated to Henry II a *Book of Architecture containing plans and drawings of fifty different buildings*. It was a collection of models intended to endow France with more symmetrical plans, better coordinated elements and a more orthodox use of the classical orders. The introduction defines the purpose of the work as being "to enrich and beautify still further your most prosperous realm, where so many fine and sumptuous edifices are being daily constructed that henceforth your subjects will not need to venture abroad in order to find any that surpass them." "Foreigners," in short, "can be dispensed with." The writer could not have expressed his purpose more bluntly or with greater freedom from any sense of inferiority. It only remained to make the most of a situation that permitted, as it were, a transfer of prestige. To most Frenchmen in the middle of the sixteenth century it seemed that their hour had struck.

Much the same was true of sculpture. There was no loss of vitality among those who carved wooden altars in the Rhineland or sculpted statuary in Burgundy or the Loire. Occasionally one finds works of a wholly new type being commissioned by prelates, patrons or aristocratic collectors; but for a long time the Gothic and classical traditions existed side by side. Cellini displayed his models at Fontainebleau, but his bronzes remained little more than royal eccentricities. There does not seem to have been any general acceptance of his chasings and arabesques. The man who did succeed in setting a fashion for scrollwork and richly decorated frames was Rosso, who paid more heed to the taste of Valois courtiers. By a curious counter-influence he even succeeded, in collaboration with the engraver Boyvin, in popularizing his designs in Italy. It is true that the French were, on the whole, fairly receptive of the new manner; but this may be due to the fact that in France, contrary to what is often alleged, the late Gothic style, common to the whole of northern Europe at the end of the fifteenth century, underwent a sort of internal transformation which enabled it more easily to assimilate the profusely expressive decoration that was pervading Europe between 1530 and 1540.

The countries of the Rhine and Danube showed much greater reluctance to admit the new culture; there the fusion of styles was no less productive, but more uneven. When Dürer died in 1528 he thought he had bequeathed to Germany a noble technique, based on theoretical treatises; but his successors were unworthy of him. In Austria, Bohemia, and especially Poland, the land of Canon Copernicus and the master-craftsmen of the Wawel, regional proclivities resulted in some very curious cases of cross-fertilization. The Renaissance began by being wedded to the taste of humanists and princes, but it did not long remain so. In remote districts, sometimes very belatedly, one finds local craftsmen making free with the whole gamut of classical forms to design multi-storied façades or stately monuments, often of an originality that should not be underestimated.

The diversity of sixteenth-century art is largely due to the fact that specimens of *every* style became familiar throughout Europe at about the same time. There was, for instance, a simultaneous acceptance of both the High Renaissance and the new genre of Mannerism. At places like Prague and Fontainebleau no distinction was made between Raphael and Parmigianino, between Bramante and Giulio Romano. There is food for thought in the way "new ideas were planted in Gothic soil. Stylistic developments in the sixteenth century art of northern Europe are intrinsically interesting because of this extreme complexity" (J. Bialostocki).

During the first thirty years of the sixteenth century the influence of Italy made itself felt in many ways. In the first place, artists were hungry for a copious and varied, though not always nutritious diet of new forms, very much as the Humanists had suddenly enriched the resources of language. The South exerted a powerful, even obsessive attraction on those who came to be known, with good reason, as Romanists. Beginning with Gossart and Van Orley in the time of Erasmus, they became a regular feature of Roman society. A rather special case was that of Van Scorel, who for a brief moment in 1522-1523 occupied a gratifying position in the entourage of his compatriot, Pope Hadrian VI. It was he who brought to Rome one of the most enterprising figures in this movement, Maerten Heemskerck, an expert in Roman archeology and in the sketching of ruins, and subsequently one of the Northerners commissioned to do decorations for the State entry of Charles V in 1525.

All this to-ing and fro-ing by artists was clearly for purposes of research. They were simply looking for every conceivable means of enriching their style, without any feeling that the resources of their own Northern techniques were exhausted. It was the beginning of a tradition of Italian *Wanderjahre* that has gone on ever since. About 1550 Anthonis Mor visited Rome, and it was in Italy that he copied Titian's *Danaë* for Philip II. It is surprising to find that even Pieter Bruegel traveled through central Italy and Naples, where he drew and painted panoramic landscapes. Van Mander relates that about 1570 P. Vlerick "made drawings from classical models, from Michelangelo's *Last Judgment* and from his sculpture, and that he also did a number of paintings, including an *Adoration of the Magi* with bizarre ruins and many small figures." There was such a constant stream of Romanists perfecting their technique that it would be hard to find any major artist at the end of the sixteenth century who did not make the pilgrimage to Rome. Goltzius, for instance, and Spranger derived great benefit from their contact with painters at work, in the years 1560 to 1570, on the new oratories and massive embellishments of Rome. The Northerners were invariably attracted by the classical feeling for composition and variety of form.

Conversely, Italian art at this time was by no means indifferent to the contribution from the North; nor, for that matter, had it ever been. As early as the fifteenth century there had been far more reciprocity than is generally realized; and once the zenith of the High Renaissance is reached and passed, there can be no question of interpreting the history of art in any terms other than those of a dynamic and fruitful polarization between North and South. Nothing is more characteristic of an age of tensile stress than such rivalries and borrowings of the picturesque. The fact remains that when it came to major issues no one doubted where the mastery lay. One has only to consider the gulf that divides Bronzino or, still more, Parmigianino from the greatest Northern portraitists, or Giulio Romano from Heemskerck. What mainly interested Italians in Northern art was technical detail: its richness of texture and luminescence; occasionally its outlandish inspiration or some element of fantasy, freakishness or extravagance. For the rest, there was no disputing Italy's position as the creator of a complete and finished art.

Those who were most keenly aware of Italian pre-eminence rejected the whole of Flemish art as being the product of a paltry and spurious aestheticism. This was the view advanced, with respect to *ideal beauty*, in a celebrated passage by Michelangelo. His words were recorded with what appears to be reasonable accuracy by the Portuguese, Francisco de Hollanda, and they are still worth quoting, for they contain the clue to the problem of North versus South.

"A pious man," Michelangelo is supposed to have said, "will derive more satisfaction from a Flemish painting than from anything produced in Italy. The latter will leave him unmoved, whereas the Flemish work will bring tears to his eyes. This is due not to the power or excellence of the picture but to the nature of the believer who contemplates it. Flemish art appeals mainly to women, especially the very young and the very old, to monks and nuns and

to certain worthy folk who have no ear for true harmony. It is an art that seeks to titillate the gaze by portraying either pleasant scenes or blameless objects such as saints and prophets. It is all frills and furbelows, tumbledown cottages, lush meadows, shady trees, bridges and streams, dignified with the name of landscapes, with lots of little figures dotted about at random. All this, though it may pass muster with some people, is really devoid of art and reason, symmetry and proportion, discernment, selection and freedom. In short, it is flaccid and inane.

"Nonetheless, there are countries where they paint worse than in Flanders. If I have been hard on Flemish painters that does not mean they are wholly bad. The trouble is, they try to excel in so many things, any of which would be difficult enough, that they fail to do any of them well."

Michelangelo, of course, was biased; for him the instinctive naturalism of the Northern masters was an abomination. But what the Italians admired in Flemish painters was not confined to insipid sentimentality and otiose prettiness. As we have seen, the sturdy execution of their portraits often had an impact on their Southern rivals (it is true, moreover, that Michelangelo and his friends disliked what they considered the inferior art of portraiture). Generally speaking there was a quality of abundance, solidity and vigor in the work of Northern artists which in the long run came into its own, when painting began to make use of authentic historical and archeological settings, of details that were true to life. Neither Giulio Romano nor Marcantonio ever did anything so massive or ironclad as Heemskerck's *Triumphs*. Flemish solidity gained in esteem as the century drew on. In 1574 one finds Zuccari declaring, according to Van Mander, that he admired Holbein's *Triumphs* in the hall of the Hansa merchants at London more than anything by Raphael.

It was harder for Northern painters to acquire elegance, spaciousness of layout and a certain brilliance and precision in portraiture. There was never a Parmigianino or a Salviati north of the Alps, not even at Fontainebleau, where Primaticcio, then Niccolò dell'Abbate, found no rivals. The currents constantly flickering between the two poles may be said in a sense to constitute the history of sixteenth-century art; and Northerners and Southerners, in so far as they were aware of this, were bound, as it were, to work out forms of compromise. One of these comes out clearly and continually in the writings of Carel van Mander, the Dutch Vasari. His *Schilderboek (Book of Painters)* of 1604 reflects a fairly general outlook: "One finds that as a rule the painters of our country have a decided preference for landscape. They have at any rate shown skill in this type of composition, whereas the Italians, while admitting that we are good at landscapes, describe themselves as masters of portraiture" (Life of Lucas Gassel). The writer goes on to quote an epigram by Lampsonius in honor of Jan van Amstel:

Propria Belgarum laus est bene pingere rura
Ausoniorum homines pingere sive deos

(The Belgians' pre-eminence is in the fine painting of landscape; the Italians' in that of men and gods.)

What one might call a stock formula would be a nude Venus by Titian, with a river flowing beside some ruins and a blue hill rising beyond it. That formula is applied, with an ingenious compromise between the prestige of the figure and the role of the landscape, in Heemskerck's *Venus* (1545, Cologne) and in Jean Cousin's *Eva Prima Pandora*. The latter, a fine painting, appears to have some connection with Henry II's entry into Paris in 1549 and may have had as its counterpart a *Lutetia Nova Pandora*; if so, it must have been intended as an allegory of Rome (Erwin Panofsky). Similarly, the *Flora* (1559) of Jan Massys seems to have been meant as an evocation of Antwerp. This image, adapted from the Italian Venuses and the Fontainebleau nymphs, and lending itself so easily to licentious overtones evocative of *Flora Meretrix*, never lost its popularity.

ROMANISM AND MANIERA FIAMMINGA

While Jean Cousin and Heemskerck may have been fascinated by the ruins of Rome, the Italians were not long in being attracted by the solid craftsmanship and extreme realism of the Northern masters. They made no secret of their interest in the singular attention to detail shown by Dürer and Lucas van Leyden, in Patinir's spellbinding naturalism, in the satanical art of Bosch. Such vivid and luminous paintings left an indelible impression, and they found their way even into Venetian collections.

It sometimes happens that an art milieu rediscovers its own inventions in the fresh light thrown on them by an outside interpretation. Lucas van Leyden's extraordinary version of Mars and Venus *in a print of 1530 is an arresting exaggeration of a distinctively Italian conception. The grimacing faces of which the Flemings were so fond re-echo the studies of facial features made by Leonardo and his followers; certain of these facial studies seem to have been made use of by Quentin Metsys, for example.*

About 1520 various features of Northern, especially German painting can be identified throughout the north of Italy. They can be seen in the Venetians who succeeded Giorgione, most conspicuously in Lorenzo Lotto, with his fondness for faces of a peculiar cast and rather blurred landscapes; in comparatively minor artists like Romanino, at Brescia, whose use of costume and gesture recalls the slashed colors of the painters of lansquenets; in Lombardy where Gaudenzio Ferrari and Luini virtually plagiarized works by Dürer and Burgkmair. The most striking examples of the trend may, however, be seen in Tuscany, despite the very different media employed. In the frescoes of the Charterhouse at Galluzzo, the long, willowy figures arranged in tiers and the emphasis on certain motifs must have derived from Northern prints. Italian patriotism, alarmed by Pontormo's beguiling example, accused him of betraying the maniera italiana e moderna, *and Vasari's biography of him (1550) contains an indictment of his complacent acceptance of "Gothic" peculiarities.*

The vogue for Flemish paintings and Northern engravings had thus become prevalent enough to annoy a good many Italians; but it was generally admitted that they had their uses. In Raphael's studio certain foreign artists had long been esteemed for their meticulous rendering of animals and foliage, which were beginning to be used in grotesques. The Italian style was bound to benefit from borrowings of this sort. At Fontainebleau there was a happy marriage of styles. Even Vasari, when he came to supervise the decoration of the Palazzo Vecchio at Florence, employed Flemings like Stradano as well as Italians like Zucchi, whose work was similar to that of the Antwerp school.

JAN MASSYS OR METSYS (1505-1575). FLORA, 1559. KUNSTHALLE, HAMBURG.

BERNARDINO LUINI (1475-1532). VENUS, SHORTLY AFTER 1525.
NATIONAL GALLERY OF ART, WASHINGTON, D.C. SAMUEL H. KRESS COLLECTION.

THE MASTER OF FLORA (ACTIVE ABOUT 1540-1560). THE BIRTH OF CUPID, ABOUT 1560. THE METROPOLITAN MUSEUM OF ART, NEW YORK.

NALDINI (BATTISTA DEGLI INNOCENTI, 1537-1591). THE GATHERING OF AMBERGRIS, 1570-1573.
STUDIOLO DEL PALAZZO VECCHIO, FLORENCE.

MORETTO DA BRESCIA (ABOUT 1498-1554). ELIJAH WOKEN BY THE ANGEL, 1522. CHURCH OF SAN GIOVANNI EVANGELISTA, BRESCIA.

PIETER BRUEGEL (ABOUT 1525-1569). THE BATTLE OF THE ISRAELITES

74

LUCAS VAN LEYDEN (1494?-1533). MARS, VENUS AND CUPID, 1530. PRINT. RIJKSPRENTENKABINET, RIJKSMUSEUM, AMSTERDAM.

THE REVOLUTION IN ENGRAVING

To grasp the variety and detail of the exchanges between North and South one is compelled to assume the existence of a further element, a channel of communication whereby frontiers could be swiftly crossed and the imagination of artists quickened. This we have already encountered in the form of engraving, which constituted an entirely new field of artistic activity. Drawing became the instrument of explorers whose discoveries were mapped by the print-maker and could thus be multiplied at will. This was a development of capital importance: it came about mainly between the advent of Marcantonio and Ghisi in Italy, corresponding to Dürer and Lucas van Leyden in the North, and the organization thirty years later of the influential print-makers' workshops at Antwerp and at Rome.

No account of the rise and diffusion of the print can be complete or even coherent unless it embraces, in a single view, the activities of engravers both in northern Europe and Italy, for there was a continual interflow of ideas and motifs. Dürer was a few years older than Marcantonio; one died in 1528, the other in 1534. Between them, they left behind a repertory of models that were taken up in every art center of any importance.

Dürer was both painter and engraver. He painted a large picture of *Adam and Eve* in which he carefully observed the Italian idea of perfect proportions. His engraving of the same subject, evoking the leafy depths of the forest and the animals lurking there, remains the more arresting image of the two. Marcantonio Raimondi was trained as a painter in Bologna but specialized in engraving after a close study of Dürer's prints (which on occasion he plagiarized). Rivaled only by Ghisi, he became the accredited print-maker of the school of Raphael, then of Giulio Romano, reproducing and popularizing their works. He thereby gained a very high reputation, quite justified by the firmness of his style. To that reputation a certain notoriety was added by the publication in 1526 of Giulio Romano's illustrations, engraved by Marcantonio, for a series of lewd sonnets by Aretino.

It is not always easy to determine the print-maker's own share in the invention and execution; this remains true throughout the century. While Marcantonio was an executant rather than a creator, Lucas van Leyden, his exact contemporary, stands out as an inventor. To the dignity of Dürer's forms he adds an acute and penetrating vision which entitles him to a high rank among the engravers of his time. He was thoroughly familiar with the work of his Italian contemporaries and predecessors, and shows it in his compositions with many figures, distributed in space with easy mastery thanks to an impeccable technique.

Woodcuts and copperplate engravings were the two techniques practised in about equal measure in the engravers' workshops, the first serving as book illustrations, the second being issued as independent sheets often forming elaborate sequences. In the 1540s there was a large output of prints in Western Europe. From 1546 to 1555 Duvet, an isolated French engraver, but an inspired one, composed his singular Apocalypse series; it was published at Lyons in 1561. The Lyonese illustrator Jean de Gourmont was capable of some highly original work. The Flemish workshops were many and prolific: the Wiericx brothers alone turned out over three thousand prints. The same high quality was maintained at the end of the century in the large figures of Goltzius, and at the turn of the century in the singular prints of Bellange.

It is not so much the aesthetic merits of these engravings that interest us here as the decisive part they played not only in the evolution but in the definition of styles. In the first place the print facilitated infinitely more long-distance contacts than had ever been possible by means of paintings or goldsmith's work. The print was intimately connected with the originality of the sixteenth century and with the emergence of what has been called "European Mannerism" (Jean Adhémar). It acted in two ways as a catalysing agent. First, by reducing every style to its linear principle, it made it readily adaptable to other media: majolica, reliefs, tapestry, armor, frescoes, easel pictures. Secondly, it provided every artist with a kind of museum in miniature enabling him to lift any motif from its context and combine it with others of his choosing. Apart from this, it encouraged the tendency to pile on details. As the artist acquired more and more models to work from, he was increasingly tempted to load his compositions with various accessories: architectural details, figure groups, distant prospects, a prominent figure in the foreground acting as a foil to the main scene.

The tyranny of a model could be overcome by combining motifs and associating them with other forms. Borrowings were taken for granted and it became common practice to combine an idea suggested by Raphael with a pose taken from Michelangelo. The Northerners who visited Rome in ever growing numbers took home portfolios stuffed with sketches of famous paintings and monuments. The silhouettes of Raphael and the battle scenes of Giulio Romano thus became the stock-in-trade of artists everywhere. Their diffusion by means of prints explains the extraordinary success of Parmigianino's feminine types, tall, slender, willowy: everywhere, even in Venice, they had become a standard component of every style by the middle of the century.

Antiquity was a favorite source of stock motifs which could always be fitted in, to round off or enrich a scene: the Roman temple, the equestrian statue, Trajan's Column, the Colosseum. From the continual use of such elements, so easy to assemble and shuffle, there emerged a composite stage-image of ancient Rome. For the artist who was hard up for ideas, this provided an abstract and evocative setting for historical scenes or a backdrop for allegories. Through the agency of the print, a compendium of all-purpose motifs was built up and transmitted far and wide.

During the 1540s Antwerp was one of the main centers of the print-making industry; there Bruegel made engravings for Hieronymus Cock "At the Sign of the Four Winds," and the powerful publisher Christopher Plantin employed Dirk Vellert and many others. In Rome the leading engravers were Lafreri and Dupérac, who composed sets of "antiquities," just as the young Joachim Du Bellay did in a famous sonnet sequence. Other centers were now coming to the fore, notably Fontainebleau, whose importance can be fairly gauged by the prints it inspired. The compositions of Rosso, themselves the fruit of a boldly composite art, were engraved by Boyvin and Pierre Milan; Fantuzzi, whose personality is more elusive, reproduced the sophisticated, voluptuous figures of Parmigianino. Classical mythology was drawn on freely as an inexhaustible source of themes—nudes, symbols and elegant forms which artists and decorators disposed in landscapes dotted with ruins, evoking a world outside time and history where all the passions and situations of the present could be illustrated. The innovations of fashion were at once popularized, sometimes prompted, by prints. The detailed, linear technique of the engraver's art lent itself perfectly to this vein of inspiration. The great engravers were wholly in sympathy with Mannerism, of which the print became one of the permanent repositories. Thanks largely to the print, Mannerism was given a new lease of life in the 1580s and, after its splendid manifestations at the Valois court of Fontainebleau, enjoyed a final flowering in the art of Goltzius, Van Aachen and Spranger at the court of Prague.

But it was Fontainebleau that provided the richest fund of architectural forms and ornamental devices—two fields in which the engraver's imagination found an unfailing stimulus. The print rendered inestimable services to the professional decorator, and the international excellence of decorative art could never have been achieved without this medium. The rise of engraving coincided with a predilection for startling, abstract forms and patterns. Rosso's scrolls and masks were worked up and diffused from 1540 on in the engravings of Boyvin. The sets of plates issued by Cornelis Bos (1546) and Cornelis Floris are bewildering in their variety: they owe much to Fontainebleau. From that time on, Europe was flooded with prints and engravers vied with each other in inventing fantastic architecture and "surrealist" ornaments.

After 1560 works of this kind appeared in profusion along the Rhine and in eastern France: the book of *Caryatides* (about 1560) by Vredeman de Vries; the *Livre de la diversité des Termes...* (1572) by the Burgundian Hugues Sambin; the *Architectura* (1598) by W. Dietterlin, doubtless the best of them all. These volumes could, of course, be used for many things—carving furniture, embossing leather, chasing weapons—and their designs were often carried to extremes of lavishness and whimsicality. They made a profound impress on the whole period.

Within this favored sector a major type of Renaissance ornament should be singled out: the grotesque. This was no mere adjunct of the arts but a medium enthusiastically adopted by the men whose adventurous imagination so imperiously dominated the sixteenth century. Grotesques were so successful and were employed so frequently and with such curious, even striking variations that, despite many repetitions and shortcomings, they must be laid to the credit of Renaissance art as a significant inventive achievement, one that went far to enrich the "life of forms." The circumstances of their development have not yet been thoroughly explored, but this much is certain: they were kept alive and propagated by the agency of the print. Capable of assuming any form, they lent themselves to every possible use. From the panels in the Vatican Stanze to the apartments at Caprarola, from the chased work of Cellini to Jamnitzer's goblets, they undoubtedly represent a strong current in the mainstream of the arts and no other system of forms was so heavily relied on in the studios. The lyrical, sometimes epic quality of ornamental grotesques enabled the Renaissance to develop a vein of original mythology by means of wholly visual media.

3

THE POETIC OF GROTESQUES

The taste for grotesques appeared early in Rome. Raphael's studio embarked on the systematic production of fantastic ornament, based on models copied from fragments of classical frescoes and stucco-work. Such artists as Morto da Feltre (according to Vasari) and Perino del Vaga (as is evidenced by his splendid drawings) were delighted with this new form of the capriccio. In the Vatican Stanze and at the Villa Madama, where Giulio Romano was in charge of operations, everyone was busy at them: "Stuccoes framed by fine grotesques in the antique manner, full of charming conceits and the most varied and extravagant objects imaginable" (Vasari, *Life of Giovanni da Udine*, 1550).

All this led to the art of the Italian Renaissance being imbued with a fondness for the fanciful and marvelous that was to color the whole period. This development would make an absorbing study, of which hardly anything has yet been written. Even a cursory survey cannot overlook the familiar passage from Cellini in which he admirably conveys the ferment caused among Roman artists by questions of ornamentation. About 1523 the youthful Cellini was trying to make a name for himself in Rome. He had been studying Islamic damascene designs, which he found unsatisfactory, and he goes on to say: "In Italy we have many types of scrolls." He mentions the Lombard volutes of ivy and the

GIULIO ROMANO (1499-1546).
THE STONING OF ST STEPHEN
(DETAIL), 1522-1523.
CHURCH OF SAN STEFANO, GENOA.

ANTOINE CARON (1521-1599). THE MASSACRES OF THE TRIUMVIRATE, 1566. LOUVRE, PARIS.

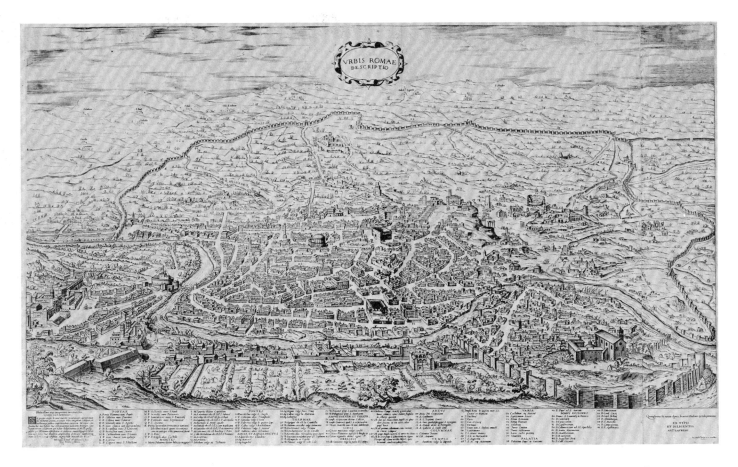

PANORAMIC VIEW OF ROME IN "SPECULUM ROMAE MAGNIFICENTIAE," PUBLISHED BY LAFRERI, ROME 1548-1586.
THE METROPOLITAN MUSEUM OF ART, NEW YORK. DICK FUND, 1941.

MAERTEN VAN HEEMSKERCK (1498-1574).
SELF-PORTRAIT IN FRONT OF THE RUINS OF THE COLOSSEUM, ROME, 1553.
FITZWILLIAM MUSEUM, CAMBRIDGE, ENGLAND.

Roman swags of acanthus "gracefully interwoven among birds and animals. They are the hallmark of good taste, and our best artists embellish these floral patterns with handsome, fanciful ornaments known to the ignorant as grotesques. The name owes its origin to the fact that the first specimens of this type of decoration were found at Rome in grottoes which had once been apartments, baths or libraries, but which had been buried by a rise in the ground level during the course of centuries." From *grotte* came the word *grotteschi*, which Cellini thought less apposite than the term *monstra* or monstrous ornament. Subsequent usage has not endorsed Cellini's suggestion, but what he says is of great importance, for it recaptures the feeling that made these designs so popular. They provided a response to a certain liking for the mysteries of nature, to which we shall have occasion to refer hereafter.

One finds the same sort of continuity between Cellini's early experiments and the armor of Leone Leoni or the elaborate beakers of Jamnitzer as may be traced between Raphael's Stanze and the Francis I gallery at Fontainebleau, or the tapestries of Bacchiacca or Arcimboldo. This sustained process of borrowing and inventiveness makes it fairly clear how various Northern devices were anticipated by the Southern imagination; for the earliest use of grotesques in Italy was contemporary with the monsters of Hieronymus Bosch. In the early stages it may well be that the Gothic taste for flourishes and droll conceits delayed the adoption of these designs by Dürer and his school. But in the decades 1540-1560 when the use of ornamental motifs was enormously developed through the agency of engravers, the Northern artists freed themselves from subjection to the Italian mode by exaggerating it to the point where it became unrecognizable. The Antwerp master Cornelis Floris, a pupil of Lambert Lombard, spent some time in Rome around 1540. Familiarizing himself with the work of Raphael, Giulio Romano and Perino del Vaga, he made some remarkable collections of grotesque designs and was mainly responsible for introducing them into Northern Europe. In manner he was less graceful, more ponderous and systematic than the master-decorators who were executing similar work at Fontainebleau.

The strained, rather neurotic style of Floris gives one a glimpse of the poetic aspect of grotesques, which may be summed up under three headings: firstly, the perpetual *negation of space* (the ornament is a microcosm, an impossible, looking-glass world); secondly, the preponderance of the *hybrid* (the ornament is peopled with morbid metamorphoses, product of a mad vitality that the mind cannot fathom); and thirdly, emphasis on the inorganic and *animation of the setting* by means of strapwork *(Rollwerk)*, scrolls, soft fleshy mouths, ready to open or to snap shut. From scrollwork it was only a step to masks; from clusters of spears to statues and architecture. The freedom resulting from the new manner can clearly be seen in the work of Floris—not that he always deserves the credit for it. The most striking paradox is that grotesques were one of the most fruitful legacies bequeathed by the Mediterranean to the North. There is no doubt that the clue to the all-important generalization of Mannerism is to be found in this new type of artistic exchange and the consequent predilection for the more exotic forms of ornament *(or monstra)*. And one can better understand the successive renewals of Mannerism in the years 1580-1590, with the publication of compilations on architecture in which those ornaments figured prominently, and in the opening years of the seventeenth century when the artists of Northern and Central Europe took so enthusiastically to Mannerism, just as the Italians were forsaking it.

GROTESQUES BY CORNELIS FLORIS IN "VEELDERLEY VERANDERINGHE"
(FOLIOS C AND F), ANTWERP 1556. ALBERTINA, VIENNA.

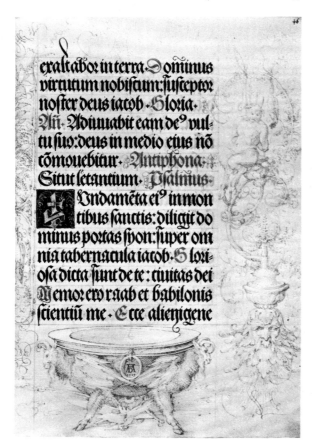

PSALM 87 IN THE PRAYER BOOK OF MAXIMILIAN, 1513,
ILLUSTRATED BY DÜRER.
BAYERISCHE STAATSBIBLIOTHEK, MUNICH.

GROTESQUES BY CORNELIS FLORIS
IN "VEELDERLEY NIEWE INVENTIEN,"
ANTWERP 1557. ALBERTINA, VIENNA.

GIOVANNI DA UDINE (1487-1564). STUCCO DECORATION WITH GROTESQUES IN THE CEILING
OF A NICHE IN THE MAIN HALL, VILLA MADAMA, ROME. AFTER 1516.

GIULIO ROMANO (1499-1546) AND GIOVANNI DA UDINE (1487-1564).
CEILING PAINTINGS AND STUCCOES IN THE MAIN HALL, VILLA MADAMA, ROME. AFTER 1516.

FORCE OF STYLE: THE INHERITORS

The expression "Renaissance of the arts" has been frequently criticized. Yet it has been handed down by tradition, and one can confidently assert that it is thankfully retained by those for whom academic distinctions have less appeal than the depth and richness of meaning to be found in words that have been minted by the complex, infinite processes of history.

LOUIS DIMIER, in *Les Arts*, October 1905.

It was common knowledge among sixteenth-century connoisseurs that Parmigianino's *Madonna of the Rose*, painted about 1530, had been copied at least fifty times by artists from all over Europe. Never, perhaps, had the work of masters been more closely studied than it was at this period in Italy. The habit of doing so gradually spread to other countries, with the same results, and the sixteenth century was an age when painters never wearied of strenuously reiterating, echoing, recapitulating what the masters had achieved.

The words of Parmigianino's contemporaries, moreover, enable one to see even more clearly why he enjoyed such immense popularity: "When people saw this young artist, as refined, friendly and courteous as Raphael himself, and when they realized how keenly he strove to emulate his master in everything, and especially in his pictures, they said Raphael's soul must have entered Francesco's body" (Vasari, *Life of Parmigianino*, 1568). Indeed the new master, whose works attracted such wide attention, was not in the least diminished by the fact that he was regarded as *Raphael redivivus*. The position of Pontormo in relation to Michelangelo had something of the same quality. An artist's standing was strengthened rather than shaken by the closeness with which his name was linked to one of those princes of the arts whose fame was already secure.

The Renaissance bestowed on its great masters, Raphael, Michelangelo and Titian, the accolade of finality, so that those who came after merely labored within the circle they had drawn. Although this belief was held mainly in Italy and Rome itself, it also conquered the North, so that before long there was a Michelangelo cult in France and a Raphael cult in Flanders. When a young painter from Antwerp or Paris crossed the Alps he succumbed to the spell of the land of the arts and began laboriously to copy what he found there. What he produced varied immensely according to his origin and persuasion; but that is another question.

It is more than a hundred years since Burckhardt analysed the new conditions of art in terms so percipient that one need only repeat them. His account gains in relevance from the fact that it is taken in part from writers of the time. Historians like Vasari and pundits like Doni seem to have had no qualms in extolling a technique that had now mastered every possible resource. Burckhardt called it the age of the inheritors, for the whole situation was transformed. "All local and corporate ties were broken. The hierarchy of Church and State required the decoration of their buildings to be monumental, imposing, often colossal. Commissions which had taxed Raphael and Michelangelo to the limit were now awarded to the first comer." When there were so many models to choose from an artist could only distinguish himself by the energy with which he exploited them. Speed of execution and extravagance of effect did him honor and proved that he was up-to-date.

Here Vasari is most revealing in the way he naïvely records his satisfaction and expounds his methods. His autobiography sets out the carefully planned stages of a successful career and the various stratagems he devised. "I can truly say," he assures us, "that I always completed my paintings, drawings and plans. I did so, whatever their merit, not only with extreme rapidity but with really unbelievable facility and effortlessness." The contradiction between this slapdash dexterity *(sprezzatura)* and careful study of the masters was more apparent than real. Vasari describes the special pains he took, when painting the *Madonna of the Immaculate Conception*, to assemble iconographic and stylistic data. The fact remains that a painter was expected to show his mettle, a certain frenzy or furor being regarded as proof of zeal and the ability to complete his work forthwith. Vasari was rather pleased with himself at having taken only a few weeks to decorate the great Farnese hall of the Cancelleria (Salone dei Cento Giorni). This eagerness to please and astonish the public is reminiscent of a prize-winning competition.

Many artists, such as Bandinelli and Cellini, forsook all dignity and were guilty of eccentricity in their desire to win favor. Their generation has been rightly accused of facile, meretricious work and of playing to the gallery in their pursuit, to quote Burckhardt once more, "of what has always attracted the crowd—luxuriance, dash and a speaking likeness." One can see what the historian was thinking of in the works of Giulio Romano, Perino del Vaga, and the brothers Zuccari: the piling on of effects, the catch-penny treatment of color, the mingling of prosaic realism with details calculated to show off the artist's skill. They acquired the habit of giving a trompe-l'œil distinctness to "certain isolated features which stood out against the pomp and bombast of the composition as a whole." This may be seen in the great hall of the Palazzo Farnese, in the San Michele chamber by Salviati at the Castel Sant'Angelo, in the decorations at Caprarola or in the French châteaux.

The fact remains that there are far too many interesting examples of such behavior for us not to try to understand it a little better. In a classically-minded historian like Burckhardt one detects the shudder of a man of sensibility when confronted by the aberrations of decadence. Wölfflin and Berenson felt the same revulsion, and it has taken a major transformation of taste for us to overcome, if only out of curiosity, this depreciatory attitude. It is now fairly evident that the impact of High Renaissance values on the development of European art was not quite what it seemed to be. The transition from the great prototypes of Raphael and Michelangelo to the recipes of Pontormo and Giulio Romano was not solely a process of decadence. Certain original features could only emerge by reason of the artistic canons that had preceded them. The Renaissance had entered a reversionary phase, characterized by the art of *maniera*. That was the true relationship of Giulio Romano to Raphael (E. H. Gombrich, 1935).

In the final analysis one must determine the attitude of these later painters towards their masters. Was it one of almost degrading servility, as Burckhardt supposed, or was it, according to the latest school of thought, one of calculated revolt? It is hard to believe that an age which strenuously championed the ideas of inspiration *(furor)*, creative talent *(invenzione)* and imaginative freedom *(capriccio)* should have done so purely in order to conceal the inadequacy or malaise of its artists. One must try, without getting embroiled in the current controversy over Mannerism, to throw light on the new issues raised by the question of style.

The principal arena is Rome shortly after Raphael's death in the spring of 1520. The army of his disciples held the field unchallenged. Michelangelo was working at Florence on the Medicean tombs in the church of San Lorenzo. Correggio at Parma and Titian at Venice were wholly absorbed in techniques of color and in achieving more sensual effects than those of the Roman and Florentine masters. The younger generation were all agog, and the whole period was filled with a strange but unmistakable ferment that was later to permeate western Europe. A hint of this is given by Vasari in a passage whose importance has lately been pointed out. A minor painter from Arezzo was brought to Rome in 1524-1525 by Clement VII's secretary, and there "he made friends with Perino, Rosso and others, and he came to know Giulio Romano and Bastiano Veneziano, as well as Parmigianino, who happened to be Rome" *(Life of Giovan Antonio Lappoli, 1568)*. The fact that all these prominent figures were there at the same time enables one to visualize Rome in the 1520s, before the siege and catastrophe of 1527, as a forcing-house of many styles. This was what Rome was to be again at the beginning of the seventeenth century, and Paris three hundred years later. There is no lack of witnesses. Cellini, for instance: "At that time (1523-1524) I used to go sketching either in Michelangelo's chapel or in the villa of the Sienese, Agostino Chigi, where I found many remarkable paintings by the illustrious Raphael. The Chigis were very proud that young artists like myself should come to them in search of subjects for study" *(Memoirs I, 6)*. The Sistine Chapel and the Villa Chigi (Farnesina) were the Mecca of sixteenth-century pilgrims. Those supreme exemplars created a clash of temperament and ambition from which many unlooked-for decisions were to follow.

At the cost of some over-simplification and setting aside the work of Pontormo and a few Tuscans, one can identify the two dominant styles of the years 1520-1530 as being an antithesis brought about by the use in different proportions of techniques whose origin can be traced in both cases to Raphael and Michelangelo. The various artists who forgathered in Rome help us to see how these two styles arose. The calamities of 1527 led to a general *sauve qui peut*. Perino was taken prisoner by the German mercenaries who sacked Rome. Rosso fled to Venice and in 1530 took service under Francis I, where he was soon joined by the painter known as Primaticcio, who had worked with Giulio Romano at Mantua. This association was to have great significance, for representatives of the two principal Italian movements now found themselves in new and highly amenable surroundings. It was not long before the authoritative Primaticcio and Rosso made their mark, adding luster to the new style with the Ulysses and Francis I galleries. This conjunction of circumstances, so providential for France, is a climacteric in sixteenth-century art, the most fruitful after the great emancipating movement of the 1520s.

During these critical years it is easy to discern two tendencies that were outstandingly meaningful and pregnant with future possibilities: the graceful manner *(venustà)*, aiming at sensuous delicacy, and the violent manner *(terribilità)*, which sought to express the artist's will. The two styles may be fairly accurately dated as following hard on the heels of Raphael, and they are represented by two great contrasting figures: Parmigianino and Giulio Romano. It is difficult, however, to account for their emergence without going into considerable detail and recalling the extraordinary direction taken by Raphael's ambition after about 1515. At that time one finds him making far more extensive use of assistants and delegating more and more tasks to them. This is true of the *Cupid and Psyche* ceiling in the Farnesina, of the Vatican Loggie, of the vast Stanza di Costantino in the Vatican, of the decorations for the villa of Cardinal Giulio de' Medici, later Clement VII. Raphael's presence imposed an astonishing degree of unity on the most variegated effects: sensuality in the Venetian mode, rhetoric in the grand manner, virtuosity in décor and surroundings. In Raphael's last works, though, such as the *Transfiguration,* his celebrated harmony came close to breaking-point.

When he died latent conflicts rose to the surface and it was as if his disciples, losing their sense of proportion, suddenly decided each to go his own way. Within a few years Giulio Romano developed a tempestuous style, wholly indifferent to beauty, such as can be seen in the fantastic ruins of his *Holy Family* in the church of Santa Maria dell'Anima, or in the *Stoning of St Stephen* which he painted for the church of San Stefano at Genoa. Although these works echo some of Raphael's figures, the style is weird and provocative, as if he were trying to rid himself of an incubus. In 1525 he moved to Mantua, where in the Palazzo del Te he had a free hand to indulge his tumultuous, highly inventive manner.

The men whom Raphael attracted to his studio were not docile supernumeraries; they must have been strong personalities, and their Diaspora led to general emergence of new talent. Even before Mantua gave Giulio Romano the means to do himself justice, Polidoro da Caravaggio had gone to Naples, where he imported the grand manner into the South of Italy. Perino del Vaga, who in 1525 had embarked on a dashing scheme for the church of Trinità dei Monti, was caught up in the confusion of the siege of Rome and the German occupation. At the end of 1527 he went to Genoa where he entered the service of Andrea Doria, for whom Montorsoli was building a palace worthy of his prestige as admiral and statesman. When it came to decorating the Palazzo Doria, the heroic style was the order of the day. One of the ceiling paintings by Perino depicts the *Shipwreck of Aeneas*: here was a pretext for prominently displaying the figure of Neptune, the sea god, just as Doria was a sea lord. Another hall was adorned with Triumphs, replete with memories of Mantegna and Garofalo. The ceiling of a third room was covered with a formidable *Fall of the Giants,* with Zeus crushing turbaned rebels of a vaguely Oriental cast, just as Doria had crushed the Turks in 1535. The powerful gyration of forms and the dramatic foreshortenings of the battle scene show that Perino modeled himself on the *terribilità* of Giulio Romano. It was characteristic of the new methods that Perino, who returned to Rome in 1538 and worked on the Castel Sant'Angelo, possessed a large collection of drawings. Vasari says that among them was a complete facsimile of Michelangelo's chapel. The *Last Judgment,* of course (1535-1541), had by the middle of the century become all-important. Though wholly foreign to Raphael's ideas, it was calculated to enthral painters like Giulio Romano and Perino del Vaga who had adopted the dramatic style. The fact that they lavished so much attention on it shows how the schools of Raphael and Michelangelo had finally coalesced.

No one would have expected this in 1515, when the whole of Rome was fascinated by the conflict between the two groups. Although Michelangelo was absent, he was in a sense represented by Sebastiano del Piombo who was known never to do anything without instructions and designs from his master. Thirty years later Michelangelo had gained the upper hand, and it seemed as if his Cyclopean style had imparted to the expressionist technique of Raphael's followers an assurance they had previously lacked. Michelangelo, in fact, had always been in the habit of making careful drawings and giving them to his pupils to paint from; or else they would sometimes use less finished sketches *(cartonetti)* after the master had done with them. Pontormo's *Venus,* Sebastiano del Piombo's *Pietà* at Viterbo, the many works by Marcello Venusti, Salviati, Giulio Clovio—all these are the product of a slightly disconcerting process whereby the inspiration of genius was transmitted to the acolyte who captured it at one remove. With Raphael it was the other way round, and the results were rather distressing. Painters exhausted themselves in trying to tread where the master had trod; witness the flagging powers of Daniele da Volterra and the tragedy of Pontormo (Johannes Wilde, 1959).

In the Rome of 1520-1525, whither every trend was converging, it is interesting to find simultaneously the Florentine Rosso and the Parmesan Francesco Mazzola, better known as Parmigianino. Rosso was a pupil of Andrea del Sarto and his *Descent from the Cross* at Volterra (1521) had shown his marked originality and a taste for syncopated rhythm and strident color. Indeed he sometimes alarmed his patrons by the strange, almost demoniacal appearance of his figures. In 1530 his brilliant, headstrong temperament caused him to try his luck in France, at Fontainebleau. He left behind him at Florence a fellow-worker in Andrea del Sarto's studio, who like himself had broken away from the gentle manner. This was the amazing Pontormo, who had painted the superb lyrical fresco at Poggio a Caiano (1520-1522) before going to the Certosa of

Val d'Ema, where he derived inspiration from Northern engravings. His fondness for etiolated figures and extremely complex yet harmoniously designed compositions naturally inclined him to model himself on Michelangelo. Yet he remained in Florence and was one of the few artists of the younger generation who did not feel the magnetism of Rome. Pontormo felt, however, the fascination of the master of the Sistine Chapel and the *Last Judgment*. His close study of Michelangelo led him to an extraordinary manipulation of the athletic nude, treated as an emblem or symbol of human emotions But, differing in this from Giulio Romano and all who followed in the path of Raphael, he never set his figures in an archaeological context. The idealization of the human figure for its own sake is characteristic of the Tuscan masters.

The recent cleaning of Parmigianino's ingenious and exquisite frescoes in the church of San Giovanni Evangelista at Parma has shown conclusively that Rome cast her spell on him when, as a young pupil of Correggio, he worked in the city for several months. It was there in fact that he found himself. He in turn made a great impression on the Romans, and the suave lucidity of his painting, apparent in his *Marriage of St Catherine* and *Vision of St Jerome* (1524-1527) caused him to be hailed as a second Raphael. But with the self-conscious art of Parmigianino takes place the decisive transition towards Mannerism: the "noble harmony" of classicism gives way to a haunting sense of unreality. His colors, now smooth and glossy, now thin and flickering, illumine remote and elegant figures. The *Portrait of a Lady* (known in the nineteenth century as the *Turkish Slave*), which he painted in Rome about 1530, is notable for this rather acidulated delicacy of tone. His fondness for willowy figures, the *figura serpentinata* of the Italians, may surely be ascribed to his familiarity with the drawings of Michelangelo, whose melodious purity of line he must have appreciated as thoroughly as did Pontormo. After his return to Parma there only remained to him ten years of feverish activity, during which he produced that most disturbing collection of exquisite Madonnas, all dressed in the height of fashion, which were immediately publicized in the form of prints and evoked admiration even in Venice and Flanders. There is no doubt that it was Parmigianino who quickened the sixteenth century with the thrill of modernity.

TERRIBILITÀ

The attraction of gigantic forms and swirling, explosive compositions was felt well before 1540 and such notable examples as Michelangelo's Last Judgment *and his Cappella Paolina frescoes. In fact the taste for surging, intertangled figure groups can be traced back to the Stanza di Costantino in the Vatican decorated by Raphael and his assistants. And behind this welter of figures—which became the inspiration of the history painters of the classical age—loomed the strange shadow of Leonardo's* Battle of Anghiari, *begun for the Palazzo Vecchio in Florence in 1504 but abandoned in 1506; one cannot help remembering too how much, during his last years in Italy and his visit to Rome, Leonardo's imagination was preoccupied with cataclysms. So the terrible scenes which were to become so rife in Italian and all European art do not derive solely from Raphael's studio and the Roman taste for powerful effects.*

Such scenes appear at the same time in the North. The altarpiece of the Virtue of Patience, which evokes the tribulations of Job and shows a stately palace crashing down, was painted by Van Orley in 1521 for the castle of Margaret of Austria at Hoogstraeten; the ornamental motifs and sharp foreshortenings have precedents in Filippino Lippi, Signorelli and certain Lombard masters. "Keep abreast of the times" was a motto that the artist seems to have taken to heart, and the quest of the spectacular was a sure way of doing so. Van Orley's pupil, the inquisitive and sometimes racy Pieter Coecke, thought so too. He displayed his powers as a stage-designer in organizing the State entry of Charles V and his son Philip into Antwerp in 1549, and also in his great series of nine tapestries, begun about 1535, illustrating the life of St Paul. Here, within a space dislocated by continually shifting levels, one recognizes the asymmetries and contrasts, and the forceful impetus, here even more tumultuous, of the tapestries designed by Raphael illustrating the Acts of the Apostles.

The Hall of the Giants in the Palazzo del Te, finished in time to be shown to Charles V during his visit to Mantua in November 1532, was genuinely admired for its "cyclorama" effect (to use the expression of F. Hartt) : a whole room was given up to an overpowering vision of battling and falling giants. Here was trompe-l'œil at its most impressive, but also at its most inane—a self-defeating masterpiece of trumpery terror effects. But no doubt political implications could be read into it. The symbol of a giant vanquished would gratify the pride of authority. Nature and power would thus seem to make common cause.

At Genoa, following in the steps of Giulio Romano, Perino del Vaga decorated the Palazzo Andrea Doria with his formidable Battle of the Giants in which Zeus crushes a crowd of turbaned rebels of a somewhat Oriental cast, just as Admiral Doria had crushed the Turks in 1535. The powerful gyration of forms, the foreshortenings and the insistence on detail show that Perino had espoused the "terrible" style. He was not to be soon forgotten at Genoa. His tours de force bore fruit a century later in the extraordinary illusionist ceilings painted in the Baroque palaces of the city by Piola, de Ferrari and Carlone. But even in the more immediate future they stimulated the verve of Luca Cambiaso, who covered the ceiling in the main hall of the Palazzo Antonia Doria (today the town hall) with a wild cavalry battle, whose casualties sprawl above the heads of visitors.

This infatuation with the gigantic took its most arresting form in the monstrous statues set up in parks to serve as a foil to shade trees and fountains. Allegories of rivers and reclining gods or goddesses from the classical repertory appear in the manner of Polyphemus above the grotto of the villa at Pratolino : they came as a last shock to the stroller, after the variously playing fountains, the disconcerting automata, the galleries haunted by nymphs. Now it is not the terror of political power that they suggest, but the panic fear of nature's overflowing vitality.

PIETER COECKE (PIETER VAN AELST, 1502-1550). THE ARREST OF ST PAUL, ABOUT 1535. TAPESTRY.
BAYERISCHES MUSEUM, MUNICH.

GIULIO ROMANO (1499-1546). A GIANT OVERWHELMED, ABOUT 1530-1532.
DETAIL OF THE FRESCO IN THE SALA DEI GIGANTI, PALAZZO DEL TE, MANTUA.

GIOVANNI DA BOLOGNA (1529-1608). GIGANTIC STATUE: ALLEGORY OF THE APENNINES, 1569-1581.
H. R. H. PRINCE PAUL OF YUGOSLAVIA, VILLA DEMIDOFF, PRATOLINO (FLORENCE).

PERINO DEL VAGA (1501-1547). THE BATTLE OF THE GIANTS, ABOUT 1530. FRESCO, PALAZZO DORIA-PAMPHILJ, GENOA.

BERNARD VAN ORLEY (ABOUT 1488-1541). THE HOUSE FALLING IN ON JOB'S CHILDREN AS THEY SIT FEASTING, 1521.
CENTRAL PANEL, ALTARPIECE OF THE VIRTUE OF PATIENCE. MUSÉES ROYAUX DES BEAUX-ARTS, BRUSSELS.

A recent cleaning of Parmigianino's attractive picture of a woman, painted in Rome about 1530, has revealed it to be not a "Turkish Slave" (the traditional title of the painting) but a straightforward portrait of a lady dressed in what was then the height of fashion. Her elaborate coiffure is held in place by a hair-net in the form of a turban; pinned to it is a curious medallion representing Pegasus. The faintly acid tones of her gown discreetly set off the round pink face. For all the charm of the portrait, there is a touch of irony in it. This winning figure, perhaps a little over-suave, is as far removed from the chaste beauty of Raphael's female portraits as Rosso's Dead Christ with Angels *(Boston) is from the poignant beauty of the Christ in the* Entombment *(National Gallery, London) by a painter close to Michelangelo. Like so many pictures by Rosso, the Boston* Christ *has something equivocal about it, in spite of all it owes to the nude figures of sarcophagus-altars and sculptured torches. The voluptuous insistence on smooth, gleaming limbs lures all the painters of this family into the pitfalls of an over-exquisite art. Not a painting by Correggio but savors of sensual indulgence. In redesigning the abbess's apartment (Camera di San Paolo) in the convent of San Paolo at Parma, so as to raise a kind of leafwork pergola, Correggio contrived some highly effective ornamental touches: the* putti *in the small round windows (given the unexpected form of medallions), and above all the play of lights casting mauve shadows and delicate reflections over the painted reliefs in the lunettes. The effect is so engaging that one almost fails to notice how short and stocky these figures are—quite different from the type of figure that was soon to hold sway in Mannerist art. The latter called for sharply silhouetted figures, a graceful play of hands, lightly swept tracts of color, all of which is well exemplified in Primaticcio's* Ulysses and Penelope, *a theme suggested to him no doubt by one of the scenes in the main gallery at Fontainebleau.*

PARMIGIANINO (1503-1540). PORTRAIT OF A LADY, 1530-1531. GALLERIA NAZIONALE, PARMA.

GIOVANNI BATTISTA ROSSO (1494-1540). DEAD CHRIST WITH ANGELS, ABOUT 1527.
COURTESY MUSEUM OF FINE ARTS, BOSTON (CHARLES P. KLING FUND).

FRANCESCO PRIMATICCIO (1504-1570). ULYSSES AND PENELOPE, ABOUT 1560.
THE TOLEDO MUSEUM OF ART, TOLEDO, OHIO. GIFT OF EDWARD DRUMMOND LIBBEY.

CORREGGIO (ABOUT 1489-1534). LUNETTE WITH SATYR, 1519-1520.
DETAIL OF THE FRESCOES IN THE CONVENT OF SAN PAOLO, PARMA.

THE PRIMACY OF ORNAMENT

In the time of Leo X the young pupil of Perugino who had made his name while still in his twenties by decorating the Vatican Stanze became in effect a kind of director-general of the arts in Rome. During the last years of his brief career, which ended in 1520, Raphael was to assume an amazing variety of responsibilities. His style gained steadily in breadth and sweep. The vast cycle of the *Battle of Constantine* in the last of the Stanze, finished by his assistants and marked above all by the hand of Giulio Romano, was followed by the gigantic tapestry cartoons with scenes from the Acts of the Apostles, which were sent to Brussels to be woven; their magnificent borders were as epoch-making as the scenes themselves. In the villa of Cardinal Giulio de' Medici, on the slopes of Monte Mario, Raphael planned a grandiose architectural composition, filling the great central loggia with fresh, graceful designs in stucco, adorned with flourishes and grotesques, which were executed by Giovanni da Udine. In the decorations he designed for the Vatican Loggie, Giovanni da Udine, Gianfrancesco Penni and Giulio Romano had to cope with a new type of composition—a sequence of small pictures (in this case Bible scenes) forming part of a trompe-l'œil décor and framed in panels of grotesques. In the years 1520-1540 the school of Raphael became known throughout Italy as much for a new decorative idiom as for its harmonious treatment of figure compositions and its skill in the rendering of attitudes and gestures.

Giulio Pippi, so closely associated with the new school of decoration based in Rome that he came to be known as Giulio Romano, moved to Mantua in 1525 and entered the service of Federigo Gonzaga, son of Isabella d'Este. There, patronized by a cultivated court and an ambitious prince who had allied himself with the Emperor Charles V (for which he was rewarded in 1530 with the title of duke), Giulio Romano realized the dream of every Italian artist: to hold sway over the art life of a city, to organize its pageants and entertainments with a free hand, to redecorate its churches, to design buildings of a new type like the Palazzo del Te, being personally responsible, as sole artistic impresario, for its decorations inside and out. Giulio Romano did for Mantua something of what in the next century Le Brun did for Versailles, and his designs, like those of Louis XIV's master-painter, show all the resourcefulness of a genius who knew how to combine the grave and the gay, to beautify places intended for pleasure and amusement, to set the stage for official ceremonies, to give to everything he touched an element of surprise and boldness that bears his mark. Never had architecture, decoration and painting been so closely and successfully blended. It was a momentous achievement. The artists of this generation sought to express themselves by means of complete ensembles, in which full scope could be given to the play of ornament— and it was on this, on decorative effect, that attention was increasingly focused.

A conspicuous example is provided by Parmigianino. In the convent of San Paolo at Parma Correggio had decorated the vault of the abbess's apartment, arranging it in the form of a pergola pierced with oval medallions and resting on brightly lit lunettes: this decorative setting gave coherence and unity to an unfolding series of allegorical scenes. Taking this innovation as his starting point, Parmigianino, ten years later (beginning in 1531), decorated the Steccata at Parma in such a way that the traditional scenes seem to be no more than an accompaniment of the ornamental motifs, these being enhanced by admirable silhouettes of basket-bearing caryatids.

There are so many examples of similar effects and the development of purely ornamental forms was so widely diffused that one is impelled at this point to ask a question. The phenomenon was, of course, characteristic of the period, but in order to grasp its full significance should one not look for a certain correlation between the abstract fantasy of the decorative elements and the actual methods of delineating figures? There are cases where one seems to detect a sort of reversibility of design and image. This deserves examination as a distinguishing trait in the art of the rising generation. For instance, one of the most markedly non-classical aspects of Pontormo and Parmigianino is the weightlessness, one might almost say the lack of equipoise, of their figures. A feature common to Pontormo's lovely *Deposition* in the church of Santa Felicita in Florence and to Parmigianino's *Madonna of St Jerome* is their use of tenuous silhouettes, standing on tiptoe and seemingly unsupported. This was an attractive novelty, which in an art nourished by the masters of Rome seems to recall certain figures by Botticelli. Its elegance and dramatic value ensured it immediate popularity and a very wide range of adaptation. The basic principle was that of a pyramid standing on its apex, providing the rather disturbing appeal of balance precariously maintained. The device was admirably suited to a whole gamut of grotesques and every kind of erratic and fluid motif.

These remained in vogue a long time, in conjunction with the highly successful *figura serpentinata,* that S-shaped silhouette so strikingly employed by Michelangelo around 1530 in the group of *Hercules and Cacus* and in his *Leda*. Here the human body is treated as an ornamental figure and, conversely, the scrolls and linear incrustations, deployed above all in vertical patterns, tended to assume shapes suggestive of the human form. The same practice was taken up by other sculptors; witness the undulating, elongated nymphs of Ammanati and the double torsion of Giovanni da Bologna's muscular nudes. The latter's *Mercury* (1564) illustrates almost to extravagance this intricate and precarious combination of form, symbol and ornament—a combination turned to account thirty years later by Adriaen de Vries.

In the field of ornament pure and simple, there were two generally accepted innovations, which to some extent rivaled each other. They were, as we have seen, the *arabesque* or formal pattern dictated by an involved and rather artificial symmetry, and the *riband*, or cut-out, which gave a more metallic effect. An exact understanding of the way these ornaments functioned will enable one to see how they could be transposed into wider terms and could even be applied to the composition of a picture.

In the case of the arabesque, it found its way into painting by means of the taste for composing groups of intertwined figures. It would seem that the sixteenth century tried to symbolize this preoccupation for us by the unwonted importance it attached to the *Laocöon*, which was incessantly admired, reproduced and imitated in drawings and prints not merely as a noble specimen of pathos, but as a model of plasticity. The new style made a fetish of all those figures coiling and writhing, with their embraces and straddlings and tangled limbs. In the *Battle of Constantine* in the Vatican Stanze this technique was applied in a way that became almost obligatory for battle-pieces during the next fifty years. Rosso's *Moses defending Jethro's Daughters* (c. 1523), with its avalanche of toppling bodies, showed the method at its most effective. The success of the *figura serpentinata* was thus prepared: it may be regarded as a special application confined to silhouettes, as a brilliant outline of a more general method.

One finds painters resorting likewise to the use of cut-outs and overlays, in other words the symmetrical unfurling of sharply delineated forms. This would seem at first to be a purely ornamental device, employed in carved frames, panels, and marquetry. If one analyses certain pictorial techniques, such as gradations of tone and the treatment of light and shadow, one can detect an imponderable but definite link between the two, seemingly disparate branches of art. About 1520 the Sienese Beccafumi began to give his colors a checker-board effect by alternating shafts of light and patches of shadow. By cutting up his composition in this wilful, erratic manner he created, as it were, a series of panels among which it is by no means easy to pick out his subjects. Rosso, on the other hand, preferred a bright color-scheme to chiaroscuro; in his case the colors, instead of shading gradually into one another, are laid on in segments or successive zones, separated by sharp edges. The draperies, the nudes, the picture surface itself, become a sort of prism, and by the slab-like arrangement of his colors the artist delivers an aesthetic shock similar to that imparted by harshly fragmented decoration. In his *Deposition* at Volterra (1521) the faceted treatment is unmistakable. Italian painting, rejecting the temptations of sustained *sfumato* and the Venetian love of glowing colors, was following a path that recalls—and may, indeed, have initiated—the abstract rhythms of decoration. This manner of treating the picture surface recurs again and again throughout the century. One finds an echo of it, for instance, during the 1560s in the celebrated "cubist" style of the Genoese master Luca Cambiaso. It is most apparent in his preliminary sketches, which show how absorbed he was by the idea of a fractured, abstract construction. Meanwhile, there was a general propagation of the intermingled groups of figures conceived by Michelangelo in the *Last Judgment* and most wonderfully developed in the works of Tintoretto.

It must not be forgotten that such extreme methods were bound to arouse opposition in Italy and elsewhere. For one thing, the Venetian emphasis on smoothly blended color harmonies stood, and intended to remain, in complete contrast to this development. Even where the spell of Venice did not operate, it was to some extent relayed by the influence of Correggio. Niceties of pigmentation and shading made of the canvas a delicately woven damask, wholly at variance with the methods we have been describing. Artists, however eagerly they might adopt the *imbroglio* or arabesque, were constantly brought up short by the demand that their drawing should possess "distinction" in both senses of the word; that is to say, it should be executed gracefully and its meaning should be sufficiently clear. The huge, gnarled figures beloved of Pontormo in his last manner are not to be found in the work of his disciple, Bronzino, who may be said to have refined his master's style. His paintings derive a studied elegance from the way he set his figures apart from one another in sharp definition and used empty spaces to enhance the quality of a selected theme or detail. His example was to be followed by many others.

FRA DAMIANO (1480?-1549). WAINSCOTING PANEL FROM THE CHÂTEAU DE LA BASTIE D'URFÉ, SAINT-ÉTIENNE, FRANCE. 1545-1550.
THE METROPOLITAN MUSEUM OF ART, NEW YORK. GIFT OF THE CHILDREN OF MRS HARRY PAYNE WHITNEY, 1942.

4

DECORATION AND MARQUETRY

By the time he arrived at Fontainebleau, Rosso had shown himself to be an original, imaginative artist with a taste for the bizarre. But he had no opportunity of painting large-scale compositions. Hence the importance of Primaticcio's arrival in 1531, for besides being a skillful stucco-worker, he had been trained under Giulio Romano at Mantua. The decorative framework—elegant, ingenious, yet sober—of the Francis I gallery forms a setting admirably suited to the themes and to the building itself. Two aedicules or two large cartouches, taking the form of scalloped strapwork *(Rollwerk)*, accompany the scenes: the re-echoed motifs, the distribution of figures both within the composition and outside it, in the frame surrounding it, and the vitality of the whole establish so close a link between the two registers that, without quite interfusing, they mingle and interconnect. *Putti, ignudi,* heraldic animals and masks tie them together at every point. This is a world of moving patterns anterior to grotesques properly so called. Freakish figures and hybrids do not yet play a dominant role, but the setting has been given a high imaginative resonance thanks to the stuccoes and their delicate convolutions which enhance the varying outlines of the frames.

This formula, so well suited to the ideal of magnificence, was to be developed in France and abroad, even in Italy, but rarely with such happy

JUDITH FLEEING FROM THE CAMP OF HOLOFERNES. MARQUETRY BY G. F. DI CAPODIFERRO
FROM DESIGNS BY LORENZO LOTTO. 1523-1525. SANTA MARIA MAGGIORE, BERGAMO.

MARQUETRY BY G. F. DI CAPODIFERRO FROM DESIGNS BY
LORENZO LOTTO. 1523-1525. SANTA MARIA MAGGIORE, BERGAMO.

MARQUETRY BY FRA RAFFAELE DA BRESCIA. 1521.
SAN PETRONIO, BOLOGNA.

CORNELIS BOS (1506-1570). ORNAMENTAL ENGRAVING.
ABOUT 1540. KUNSTHALLE, HAMBURG.

PIERRE BONTEMPS (ABOUT 1506-ABOUT 1570).
MARBLE URN FOR THE HEART OF FRANCIS I. 1556.
BASILICA OF SAINT-DENIS.

JACQUES ANDROUET DU CERCEAU (ABOUT 1510-ABOUT 1585).
FONTAINEBLEAU CARTOUCHE. PRINT.
BIBLIOTHÈQUE NATIONALE, PARIS.

results. For the craze for grotesques brought a proliferation of hybrids in which the organic merged with the inorganic, the garland turned into a membrane, the gaping jaw into a bezeled block, following the recipes of Cornelis Floris. An almost demoniac type of cartouche was diffused by Cornelis Bos. The strapwork adaptable to so many uses became a favorite device with sculptors: on the urn containing the heart of Francis I, carved by Pierre Bontemps for Saint-Denis, they are treated as volutes. This led to all sorts of *trompe-l'œil* effects, as in the framework of the bays of town-houses at Toulouse, or in the Casa Leone Leoni at Milan, where the cartouche at the top of the façade becomes a kind of cage into which the victim of the two emblematic lions on the frieze is about to fall.

Another highly favored form of decoration was marquetry. Here the sixteenth-century taste for the fantastic can be gauged by comparing Quattrocento intarsia with the intricate inlays so popular in Italy and Germany after 1530. Lotto's marquetry designs for a Bergamo church contained so many small figures that the pieces of wood that went into the inlays had to be greatly multiplied. At Bologna, though richer effects were increasingly aimed at, the tradition of orderly design maintained itself: triumphal arches, architectonic structures, perspective views, still lifes, formal compositions. These inlays appealed to French taste: panels of this type were ordered from Fra Damiano for the Château de la Bastie d'Urfé, and a refectory at Le Puy was inlaid with illusionist geometric patterns.

Inlaid chests and cabinets became popular, developing into an industry which flourished above all in South Germany. The striking panels of the Wrangelschrank constitute a masterpiece of what must have been an immensely prolific craft. For the first time ornamental motifs were combined with ruins and fragments of architecture or armor to make up abstract, quite unlifelike landscapes.

Here is proof enough that figure art was being invaded and overwhelmed by decorative trends. The intention could hardly be more explicit. Endless enchantments were found in the artificial creatures of ornament. Their appeal is enshrined in sets of engravings, like Stoer's which offered models for inlaid work, then Jamnitzer's and those of other purveyors of motifs for the goldsmith and the cabinetmaker. These pattern books undoubtedly had a high speculative value for Dürer's remote followers and for Italian theorists. In practice, the demands of the middle- and upper-class clientele gradually attenuated it after 1580-1590. The Northern workshops aimed at a rich display of incrustation, setting off ebony with gold and precious stones. Incredibly lavish altars and cabinets began to appear in the great houses of Bavaria and Austria.

This was not the case in Italy where the heyday of marquetry, and of animated decorations, was over before the end of the century. The spirit of formalism remained very much alive, however, engendering the capriccios of Zuccari and many others.

There is plenty of evidence to show that purely formal sophistication was often accompanied by expressions of real imaginative power and fantasy. A curious light is thrown on this matter in a recently published work by the Renaissance architect Pirro Ligorio, who disliked and distrusted the fashions of the 1560s. He considered it disgraceful, for instance, to place a broken pediment on a church façade, for such devices are only becoming on tombs. The broken pediment, like everything else that was broken, might fittingly symbolize the blind Fury that "slits the thin-spun life," but not the fullness of God's presence. Here the writer is speaking in terms of ethical intonation; but he goes on to aim a broadside at the style then in vogue: "Let us now speak of what they call 'elongating' *(snocciolamento)*, in other words the unreasonable violence done to movements, bodies, hands, arms and thighs, and all manner of contortions calculated to give an air of frenzied movement, an attitude both repellent and demented, so that the scene is conveyed by menace rather than persuasion. Their one object is to twist and tangle their figures in such confusion that no one can make them out." Or again: "Nothing appears to them beautiful or worthy of note unless it has undergone some bizarre abridgment. Their figures sprawl in wild disarray, and what they most admire is violent foreshortening" (Pirro Ligorio, *Trattato di Architettura*, folio 12 verso, Collins, London, 1964). This attack on geometric perversions and abstract effects enables us also to see why they were so successful.

DECORATED WINDOW OF THE HOTEL DU VIEUX-RAISIN, TOULOUSE. AFTER 1550.

AUGSBURG MASTER. CHEST DECORATED WITH WOOD INLAYS, KNOWN AS THE "WRANGELSCHRANK," WITH PANELS OPEN. 1566.
LANDESMUSEUM FÜR KUNST UND KULTURGESCHICHTE, MÜNSTER.

AUGSBURG MASTER. CHEST DECORATED WITH WOOD INLAYS, KNOWN AS THE "WRANGELSCHRANK," WITH PANELS CLOSED. 1566.
LANDESMUSEUM FÜR KUNST UND KULTURGESCHICHTE, MÜNSTER.

RHETORIC

After the 1530s Rome was in sore straits. The dispersal of her artists benefited places like Genoa and Venice at her expense. It created a vacuum in Rome which coincided with the flowering of most of the other cultural centers of Europe, such as Fontainebleau, Antwerp and Seville. Yet one should not overlook what was happening to the arts in Central Italy, for it enables one to understand the early phase of Mannerism and, after 1540, the beginnings of the second phase which likewise had repercussions abroad. The reversion to a more dictatorial regime in the Church and the States owing allegiance to the Emperor created a harsh climate of anxiety and stress, in which artists tended to be much more submissive in gratifying the whims of their patrons. It would be doing the dictates of theologians and censors too much honor to say that they encouraged nobility and restraint of style; what they really aimed at was propriety in matters of detail. The artistic tone of the Counter-Reformation was marked by two characteristics which were most conspicuous about the middle of the century: a facile and eclectic triteness, which was thought suitable for inculcating a naïve piety and illustrating dogma; on the other hand, an overblown, opinionated rhetoric with all the requisite pomp for securing the privileges of those in authority.

The latter characteristic, which was the more significant, made its appearance at Rome under the aegis of Michelangelo, who had returned there in 1534, at the invitation of the Farnese Pope, Paul III. The hour of "Michelangelism" had struck. There can be no overestimating the influence of the *Last Judgment* (1535-1541), in which it would seem that he set out to efface the optimism and sublime objectivity of his earlier work on the ceiling of the Sistine Chapel. This was the apogee of *terribilità* and the birth of a new style. The rational concept of space was shattered; the nude became a means of conveying anything and everything; the inspiration was emotional, always at the stretch, keyed up by the drawing. The motifs of the *Last Judgment*, broadcast in the form of prints, became the stock-in-trade of all those Florentines, like Vasari, Daniele da Volterra, Salviati, Jacopino del Conte, who about 1540 joined in the rush of place-hunters to Rome. Their principal set-piece, the fresco of the *Deposition* in the church of Trinità dei Monti, is believed to contain the figure of Michelangelo himself. His style was now to form the main ingredient of their work, with a dash here and there of Venetian color or Raphaelesque urbanity. In this respect Salviati's vicissitudes make a more appealing object of study than the laborious contrivances of Vasari, like the altarpiece of the *Immaculate Conception*.

The first really revealing embodiment of this inspiration was in the oratory of San Giovanni Decollato, where practically all the leading followers of Michelangelo had a share in the work, aiming at an effect of tragic pathos by loosely disposing the spatial registers so as to make the most of the figures, themselves enlarged or reduced at will. In 1546, on the recommendation of Paul III, and using themes worked out by him which fancifully combined history and allegory, Vasari decorated the Chancellery: this, as we have seen, was a complete cycle of frescoes elaborately framed by a setting of simulated niches, medallions and learned inscriptions. The new style called for large ensembles, self-contained within the terms of a single over-riding theme: the triumph of Catholic piety over heresy or the proud annals of a princely family.

In Venetia the architectural designs of Sanmicheli and Palladio had fostered the taste for a stricter, more sober type of art than that of Giulio Romano.

But the interest in fresco cycles, or sequences of large canvases, closely associated with architecture remained very much alive in Venice. In 1555-1556 Paolo Veronese, taking his cue perhaps from the aerial graces of Correggio but mindful too of the Roman tradition of decoration, gave a brilliant demonstration of his powers in the church of San Sebastiano, then in the Villa Maser—frescoes full of smiling landscapes, figures hiding behind columns, and entertaining touches, all presented with convincing illusionism. Ceiling decorations had long been fashionable in Venice: some of the finest of them all were painted now by Veronese and his pupils, in the Ducal Palace, the oratories, the confraternities *(scuole)*. But a great force arose at that very time to cast its mighty shadow over an art too brilliant to be moving—Tintoretto. Through him the dramatic intensity of Michelangelo made its way into Venetian painting, then still glowing with the rich tonalities of Titian, stirred about 1545-1550 by emanations of Parmesan Mannerism, and endowed with exceptional but still largely latent powers of eloquence. These found expression in Tintoretto's surging gulfs of shadow, his fitful lights, his massive figures in turbulent depths of space. His great cycle of paintings in the Scuola di San Rocco (begun in 1564, finished in 1587) is in this respect the fulfillment of all that was promised by Michelangelo in the Cappella Paolina and one of the landmarks of sixteenth-century art.

It was just about this time that the rhetorical style formulated around 1540 flourished anew in the oratory of Santa Lucia del Gonfalone in Rome. It did not quite lose itself in the quicksands of mere artifice but tended rather to grow preposterously formal. The law of acceleration having come into full play, every painting had to blow a triumphant trumpet. There was no longer any room for modest statement, no more than there was in the writings of Ronsard, d'Aubigné, Tasso and the Elizabethans. All sense of verisimilitude had been lost, nor was it soon to be recovered. For the taste for this art was one from which people were not readily weaned, either in Rome or the North. Lombard artists, especially, clung to it for many years. It forms a major element in the work of G. B. Crespi, known as Il Cerano, who used it at the beginning of the seventeenth century when he executed the *telari* of Milan Cathedral in honor of the life and miracles of St Charles Borromeo.

Above all, however, there was a considerable influx of northern artists into Rome during the latter part of the sixteenth century. In 1570-1571 the youthful Spranger from Antwerp spent several months in the pope's service, whence he made contact with this school and retained some of its boldest ideas. Carel van Mander likewise visited Italy, followed soon after by Goltzius, Cornelis Cornelisz and others. There was, in short, a renewal of the line of development we have already noted. Painters and decorators from the North, having served an apprenticeship in Rome, took up the work of the Italians. At Prague, and later at Antwerp and Haarlem, these men were to produce the striking art of later Mannerism, in which rhetoric and conceits blended in a harmonious and beguiling synthesis. Their relation to the art of Rome in the 1570s may be likened to that between Fontainebleau and Rome fifty years earlier. The wheel had come full circle. In Central Europe and the Low Countries, however, painting vied too readily with the arts of the goldsmith and tended to covet a place in the Kunstkammer, that cabinet of curiosities where, among the prints and the clutter of bric-à-brac, the meretricious relics of Mannerism were soon accumulating. The last word of the rhetorical art of the Roman masters took the form of that cold, recherché grandiloquence which characterizes court art.

There are two conspicuous examples of large, post-Michelangelesque picture cycles in Rome in the time of Paul III (1534-1549): the frescoes in the Chancellery (Cancelleria) and in the oratory of San Giovanni Decollato at Velabro. The former sequence, carried out by Vasari as a triumph of virtuosity, is also a fine specimen of political rhetoric. There is a huge state apartment painted from end to end; a dado with staircases in trompe-l'œil*; scenes illustrating the main events of the pontificate; allegories and inscriptions wherever there was room for them. The whole affair, existing on several planes of reality, is dispatched without much inspiration, but it possesses a certain imaginative force thanks to the dynamic way in which the pictures are set in the overall scheme and the almost cinematic effect of their display.*

The oratory of the brotherhood of St John the Baptist is more interesting. Between 1538 and 1543 it was decorated with scenes from the life of the Baptist, on a general plan similar to that of the main hall in the Chancellery. In Jacopino del Conte's portrayal of the Preaching *the figures are standing in a clear, golden, almost unbroken light. In the adjoining scene of the* Baptism *an immense nude reclines in the foreground of a composition entirely filled with a casual assortment of Michelangelesque figures. On either side of the altar two magnificent saints, leaning forward, project violently into the room and seem to be hovering over it. In certain effects of this rather composite cycle one gets a foretaste of devices that were to be employed subsequently, and even of Tintoretto's stormy canvases twenty years later.*

It took about a generation for the rhetorical manner, whose beginnings we have seen, to take root and be adopted generally. During the 1560s the Tuscans began to be superseded at Rome by painters from Emilia. After 1560, in the Florence of the Medici Grand Dukes, Vasari set to work with his Flemish friends, including Stradano, and his many pupils, such as Zucchi, on the stately decorations of the Palazzo Vecchio. In his Ragionamenti *Vasari sets forth the historical, mythological and symbolical program adopted here, providing for a particular function and setting in each room and on each floor, so as to form an exhaustive ensemble. Roman themes were incorporated in the enormous battle pieces in the main hall (for which Leonardo's and Michelangelo's great battle scenes had been intended over half a century before). The elaborate, highly finished scenes in Duke Francesco's* studiolo *were given a frigid, mannered setting (1573). A generation with a more sensitive understanding of the same rhetorical style had already shown its mettle in Rome. Taddeo Zuccari had collaborated in the Villa Giulia decorations and his* Bacchanal *was one of its finest adornments; he went on to work with Vignola, at*

Caprarola, in the Farnese palace. Here, in the great hall of the Fasti Farnesienses, Zuccari deployed a would-be epic panorama of the great deeds of a powerful family. His compositions, too anecdotal and too close to history, fall short of Salviati's brilliant sequence of well-connected scenes in the Palazzo Farnese in Rome, which Michelangelo was just finishing. On the other hand, the combination of trompe-l'œil *and grotesques in the corners of the Caprarola apartments do great credit to the skill of Giovanni dei Vecchi.*

In Rome, the extraordinary oratory of Santa Lucia del Gonfalone (1569-1577), near the Via Giulia, shows how far style had changed since the San Giovanni Decollato decorations. Painted oratories had been called for by the Counter-Reformation: by around 1570 there were a number of them in Rome decorated with extensive picture cycles (Quattro Santi Coronati, Trinità dei Monti, Il Crocefisso), but artistically the Gonfalone was the most important. It is doubtless going too far to maintain that "the frescoes adorning the walls of the Gonfalone oratory lie at the source of international Mannerism, comparable in significance to those of the Sistine Chapel" (F. Zeri). The fact remains that in this ambitious scheme of decoration one finds for the last time the animation of painted façades, with an elaborate system of niches and rinceaux providing a rich setting for dramatic scenes. The latter make much of contrapposto *and emphatic foreground figures, of fugal complexity and ornamental touches. The oratory contains a* Scourging of Christ *by Federico Zuccari, Taddeo's younger brother, which Van Mander pronounced "a fine and attractive painting." There one may admire the facile, repetitious energy of Livio Agresti, based on a modified Michelangelesque style. Above all, the oratory exhibits the work of a new group of Emilian painters: Raffaellino da Reggio and Marco Pino, adepts at spatial contortions, and Bertoja, the decorator from Parma, who came to Rome in 1572 and was apparently provided by the brilliant Lelio Orsi with preparatory designs in which great violence is mingled with unexpected touches of gentleness, clearly deriving from Correggio.*

The same features mark the style of Pellegrino Tibaldi at Bologna, together with a fondness for the whimsical and bizarre. They appear too in Luca Cambiaso, a master of tricky light effects and decorations full of surging movement. These were the artists, along with Federico Zuccari, who were called in by Philip II about 1580 to decorate the library and main cloister of the Escorial. After his return to Rome, Zuccari decorated his own house at Trinità dei Monti with self-flattering allegories and homely scenes, and finally, in 1607, published a treatise in which he set forth all the tricks of the trade.

GIOVANNI DEI VECCHI (ABOUT 1536-1614). FRESCOES IN THE SALA DEGLI ANGELI, 1562. PALAZZO FARNESE, CAPRAROLA, NEAR VITERBO.

FRANCESCO SALVIATI (1510-1563). DETAIL OF THE FRESCO IN THE HALL OF THE FASTI FARNESIENSES.
MID-16TH CENTURY. PALAZZO FARNESE (FRENCH EMBASSY), ROME.

FRANCESCO SALVIATI (1510-1563). ST ANDREW, 1538-1543.
FRESCO, ORATORY OF SAN GIOVANNI DECOLLATO, ROME.

ENTRANCE WALL OF THE ORATORY OF SANTA LUCIA DEL GONFALONE, ROME,
WITH FEDERICO ZUCCARI'S "SCOURGING OF CHRIST," 1569-1577.

MARCO PINO (ABOUT 1525-1588). THE RESURRECTION, 1569-1577.
FRESCO, ORATORY OF SANTA LUCIA DEL GONFALONE, ROME.

GIOVANNI BATTISTA ROSSO (1494-1540). THE EDUCATION OF ACHILLES, ABOUT 1538.
FRESCO, GALERIE FRANÇOIS Ier, CHÂTEAU DE FONTAINEBLEAU.

TADDEO ZUCCARI (1529-1566). BACCHANAL, 1553. FRESCO, VILLA GIULIA, ROME.

JACOPINO DEL CONTE (1510-1598). SCENES OF THE LIFE OF ST JOHN THE BAPTIST, 1538-1543.
FRESCO, ORATORY OF SAN GIOVANNI DECOLLATO, ROME.

GIORGIO VASARI (1511-1574). THE LIFE OF POPE PAUL III FARNESE, 1546.
FRESCO, SALONE DEI CENTO GIORNI, PALAZZO DELLA CANCELLERIA, ROME.

III

NATURALISM
AND SYMBOLISM

COSMOS AND ARCHITECTURE

At the Renaissance there was no criterion of the impossible.
A. KOYRÉ

The philosophers of German Romanticism were fond of tracing early intimations of their *Naturphilosophie,* their unified interpretation of nature and spirit, in the writings of the Renaissance. Novalis admired Paracelsus; Schelling appealed directly to Giordano Bruno. They had some reason to regard these authors as embodying valuable relics of a non-Cartesian, non-classical philosophy, deriving as much from analogies as from concepts. Be that as it may, the well-meant attempts of Romanticism to rationalize the searching insights of the sixteenth century could only have the effect of blurring them. The Romantics at least had the merit of grasping the irrational principle of *Pansophia,* which deflected and, before Bacon, often checked the efforts of scientific thought to come into existence.

Among the most powerful currents throughout this period was a wholly original and to some extent compulsive awareness of nature as a living reality. The steady advance of cosmological speculation ran parallel to and sometimes overshadowed metaphysics. In its attempt to be both descriptive and comprehensive, it encountered the traditional affinities of philosophy: God and the World, Spirit and Nature, Invisible and Visible. It applied a strictly cosmological system to the natural species—mineral, vegetable and animal—and above all to the relationship between heaven and earth, which had become the chief concern of "physicists" as a result of the facts observed by Copernicus and his successors. In all this speculation there was a notable tendency to break the existing affinities, which were generally, like all philosophical categories, of Aristotelian and Scholastic origin: to break them, that is, extensively, by stressing the infinite diversity of phenomena, and comprehensively, by insisting on the connexity between all orders of phenomena and levels of existence.

Although the most startling consequence of Copernicus' discovery was the collapse of official geocentric dogma, a number of general philosophical inferences were likewise drawn from it. Men could more easily apprehend the harmonic structure of the planetary system and thereby the perfection and permanence of the natural order. Canon Kepler, moreover, advanced two memorable theories. Firstly, he believed that the connection between the "guiding angels" and the planetary orbits was now more apparent than ever, and that the solar system was indeed an analogue of the divine world and its unseen hierarchies. In the second place, the riddle of the *mysterium cosmographicum* could be answered not merely in terms of the musical scale, familiar to Platonic and Orphic tradition, but also by means of the interlocking of the "pure bodies," which themselves were related to musical tonality. It therefore became easier and more instinctual than ever to make a visual and graphic projection of the universe. The only change was that greater stress was laid on the thrust and rotation of energy. Finally, it should be remembered, this representation of a living cosmos was supplemented and reinforced by the mythological description of the zodiac and of the deities who symbolized the celestial powers.

Giordano Bruno was the first philosopher to adopt, or at any rate to follow up the implications of Copernican theory. In his dialogue *De l'Infinito, Universo et Mondi* he described an "infinite" universe made up of finite systems. In this he was doubtless employing an idea of Lucretius in order to convey the infinite expansion of reality and the coherence of each component unity (A. Koyré). He was thus led into a fundamental ambiguity due to his insistence on reconciling Platonism with naturalism; for he clung both to the Platonic concept of different levels of existence broadening through love into the Idea, and to that of an unlimited expansion of the energy inherent in nature. He seems often to have approached a pantheistic conclusion. His stellar universe, consisting of suns and earths, involved both a fascinating contraction in the scale of our own world and far greater proximity, amounting to downright fusion, of heaven and earth.

Bruno's attempt, however, cannot be summed up in terms of the usual dilemmas. "His vision could not be fully expressed by such antitheses" (P. O. Kristeller), except through the operation of a paradox whereby reason would be driven, from one extreme to another, towards an intuitive process of great intensity and, in the eyes of the twentieth century, extreme confusion. To the sixteenth century there was a correlation between the two concepts of a living natural order and of symbolic analogies or, in modern parlance, correspondences. This point must, as we have seen, govern any analysis of how the basic naturalism of the sixteenth century was related to its constant use of symbols. We shall now try to make the process clearer by means of morphological investigations in three distinct, totally unrelated fields: architecture, the scientific portrayal of living creatures and standards of erotic beauty.

Some of the finest creations of the sixteenth century consisted in the improvement of natural sites by means of architecture and gardens. They were ambitious compositions which have often lasted better than any others and can most vividly reveal to us at a glance the character of the period. Everything is to be found in them. The social status conferred by luxury is associated with landscaping and the novel employment of vegetation, which themselves are made more spectacular by terracing and ornamental water. There is complete freedom of architectural design, which can thus adapt itself to the whims of the exalted owner. Nothing stands in the way of his vagaries of taste, which can find expression in symbolic devices, pseudo-classical settings or allegories reflecting and befitting his zest for life. No more eloquent introduction to this subject can be found than the villas of Latium about the middle of the century: Caprarola, a fortress surmounted by a park; the Villa d'Este, composed by Pirro Ligorio of rich, mossy cadences for the Cardinal of Ferrara; the gardens of Bomarzo,

where the bent for *capriccio,* so essential to these productions, resulted in a riot of fantastic clowning. In France there is no end of striking examples, among which one may mention Anet, Fontainebleau and the Tuileries as restored by Du Cerceau.

They all had something of the prodigy about them. It set them apart from normal dwellings and we shall try to define it shortly by resorting to the concepts of festivity and display. This quality was achieved by a skillful combination of effects and, so to speak, with the connivance of Nature, tamely submitting to the whims of the great. In other words, the novelty and charm of these creations depended to a great extent on the original bringing together of natural and social factors, whereby a grandiloquent ensemble was laid out on a commanding or well-disposed site.

Within the general context of this fashion there developed a curious motif in the shape of artificial caves and buildings imitating the wilderness of a rocky landscape. The architectural use of this imitative theme says a good deal about the naturalism of the Renaissance and its predilection for evocative organisms. No one has yet written a history of the subject, as regards Italy, France or western Europe as a whole. Poems and romances contain innumerable references to caves, either as earthly paradises or as retreats of sanctity and bliss, or sometimes as dread abodes of savagery. In the fifteenth century they still played a humble part in painting and decoration; yet one can perceive a dawning awareness of these natural phenomena in a famous passage where Leonardo da Vinci alludes to the fascination of caverns, with their overpowering mixture of curiosity and terror. Subsequently, however, the main interest is to be sought in the layout of parks and villas rather than in painting. The villa of Giulio de' Medici, built by Raphael and Giulio Romano, left unfinished and completed after 1527 by the daughter of the Emperor Charles V, includes a suite of rooms imitating those of Roman baths and laid out on different levels: the terraced effect produced here, on the slopes of Monte Mario, has much in common with the extraordinary terraced site of Palestrina. The result was a sort of mixture of villa, landscape-garden and thermal grotto. There came a succession of great villas designed in the same spirit: the Villa Farnese on the Palatine, the Villa Medici on the Pincio, etc. In these, however, the Roman bath was reduced to an architectural or, more simply, artificial grotto. Such fanciful structures called for fanciful decorations.

A particularly good example is the garden laid out by Buontalenti in 1583 for the Grand Duke Francesco, with its grottoes full of surprise effects, its automata, its fountains often calculated to start playing when the visitor least expected it; on each level of the garden was some new allegory of the nymphs or Cupid (description by Richard Lassels, 1670, utilized by John Shearman, 1967). At Saint-Germain-en-Laye, at the end of the century, the Château Neuf was fitted out by the Francini with an even bolder succession of fairy-like grottoes.

The taste for such constructions spread all over Europe. The court architect of every prince and princeling was expected to create new landscapes.

One man alone seems in the plans of his villas to have stood out against the vogue for naturalism in architecture. The stately Palladio was content with the geometrical dignity of masses placed against the sky and the proper ordering of his surfaces. To him, as he said in so many words in his *Treatise,* cosmic harmony was reflected in the nobility of abstract form. But the man who built the Rotunda and Villa Maser did not confine himself to this lofty aim. He so orientated his houses that they lay along the axes of the sky, and he extended their vistas by a meticulous alignment of statues and objects. His structural purism, moreover, did not prevent him from frequently resorting to the use of bossage and rustic masonry, suggesting, in the consummate order and balance of this art, a lurking allusion to the geological origin and natural crudeness of the materials which he dominated and fashioned into architecture.

5

GROTTOES AND NATURE

When Giulio Romano decorated the Palazzo del Te he placed a *casino della grotta* in one corner of the main courtyard. It was built in the Doric mode, on a small central plan, with a garden and a loggia. There was a profusion of lunettes, terminals and stucco ornaments, shells, mosaics and figures of nymphs and fauns. The whole affair was a gem of happy allegory and light-hearted banter.

It soon found imitators, especially in France. There was an increasing vogue for mock-rusticity, combined with a taste for fountains, either playing in groups or as part of a monumental design. In Tuscany, Michelangelo's *Slaves* were placed for a while in the grotto of the Palazzo Pitti, for it was felt that a rocky wilderness provided the indispensable setting for the two controversial but much admired fragments of his unfinished masterpiece. One constantly finds evidence of the "life of forms" being linked to the life of nature. In the villa at Castello niches and grottoes were built to house casts of animals and statues by Giovanni da Bologna. In the villa that Buontalenti built at Pratolino, soon after 1565, for Francesco de' Medici, room was found for Giovanni da Bologna's colossal, craggy *Allegory of the Apennines*. Throughout the century and for generations to come, no country house was built or its gardens laid out but one of these accessories was there to show that the house was part

DRAGON FIGHTING A LION AND A LIONESS. 1552. SCULPTURE IN TUFA ROCK.
CASTLE PARK, BOMARZO, NEAR VITERBO.

ANTONIO FANTUZZI (1510?-ABOUT 1550?).
ARTIFICIAL GROTTO FOR FONTAINEBLEAU. 1545. PRINT.
BIBLIOTHÈQUE NATIONALE, PARIS.

SERLIO, "TUTTA L'OPERA D'ARCHITETTURA
ET PROSPETTIVA" (VOL. VII): RUSTIC GATE.
INSTITUT D'ART, PARIS.

GIULIO ROMANO (1499-1546).
THE CASINO DELLA GROTTA,
PALAZZO DEL TE, MANTUA.
ABOUT 1530-1531.

THE GROTTO OF THE CHÂTEAU
DE LA BASTIE D'URFÉ, NEAR SAINT-ETIENNE.
ABOUT 1548.

of the countryside, and that nature must be made to serve the owner's taste for pomp and pleasure.

This movement had considerable repercussions in the countries of northern Europe, France above all, where the advice of Southern landscape-gardeners was welcomed with enthusiasm. Charles VIII had been so impressed by the villa and the gardens of Poggio Reale at Naples, which had been seen by Peruzzi and Serlio, that he had Amboise and Blois redesigned. The Villa Madama was carefully studied, as were the Villa Medici and the Farnesina. The new taste received a further stimulus from the arrival in France of Serlio and Primaticcio, who put forward suggestions for making the most of a countryside far better endowed than Italy with forests and water. This resulted in the lakes of Fontainebleau and the canals of Anet, where, as in Tuscany, appropriate statues were disposed at strategic points. It was not long before caves and rusticity made their appearance. As early as 1540 Fontainebleau seems to have had its "pinetree grotto," with figures of Atlas rooted in the stone like living pillars, reminiscent of Michelangelo's *Slaves*.

Princes and grandees displayed even more inventiveness in planning their country seats. When the Cardinal of Bourbon completed the admirable domain of Gaillon, he placed a curious little casino-alcove on the terraces overlooking the Seine. Among the original features of La Bastie d'Urfé in the Forez, designed in 1548 by an ambassador on his return from Italy, was a grotto decorated with shell-work, adjoining the chapel and thus forming part of the building itself. Always the addition of ornamental motifs—sea-shells, stucco, mosaics, figures carved in the rock—was calculated to enhance the rustic charm of the place, as if it were the haunt of nymphs or strange fabulous creatures. It was an easy transition from naturalism to Arcadian rusticity, and the two themes were always present in the landscape-gardener's art.

To see how deeply these curious abodes affected those who built and cherished them, we can turn to a great example, as familiar to us in literature as it is now physically unrecognizable: the grotto at Meudon. It was begun in 1552 by Primaticcio, Giulio Romano's former associate at Mantua, in a fold of the hillside sloping down to the Seine. "At Meudon the Abbé Primatice executed for the Cardinal of Lorraine a host of designs in his great palace, known as the grotto. One might well call it the Thermae, both on account of its resemblance to that type of ancient edifice and because of the size and quantity of the loggie, staircases and public and private apartments it contains" (Vasari, *Life of Primaticcio*, 1568). The reference to Meudon's classical prototype, itself made familiar by the Villa Madama, is thoroughly apposite. Outside it comprised a series of terraces, with vistas and ornamental water; within there was rock-work, accompanied by a host of suitable mythological figures. The feel of the place, which was unreservedly admired, has been captured for us in an epithalamium composed by Ronsard for a great wedding in the royal family. All the features that gave Meudon its renown are eloquently evoked, and one can see how well the poetic inspiration of Primaticcio was attuned to that of Ronsard.

"While their cattle cropped the grassy plain, slowly they ascended to the grotto of Meudon, where young Charles, whose name is sacred to the woods, had built a retreat lovely enough to be the eternal dwelling of the Nine Sisters. Then they took courage and entered the hallowed, fearful cavern where, as if touched by divine fire, they felt their minds suddenly gripped by an insensate passion. They stood amazed to see so fine a building erected in such a lonely waste, with stately plan and façade and rustic pillars rivaling the grandeur of antique columns; to see how on the walls Nature had portrayed the liveliest grotesques in flinty rock; to see halls, apartments, chambers, terraces, festoons, checkered and oval designs and enamel bright with many colors..."

Vasari added to Ronsard by describing the glittering mosaics and enamel-work of the apartments. To right and left of the entrance stood Pallas Athene and Bacchus; above it was placed the dedicatory inscription: *quieti et musis*. About the same time Pirro Ligorio was landscaping for the Cardinal of Ferrara the hillside of the Villa d'Este, where the decorations included an equally lavish display of iconography. To crown the general effect, the rooms of these villas and grottoes often contained frescoes or paintings which reflected, as if in a mirror, the surrounding landscape and its amenities.

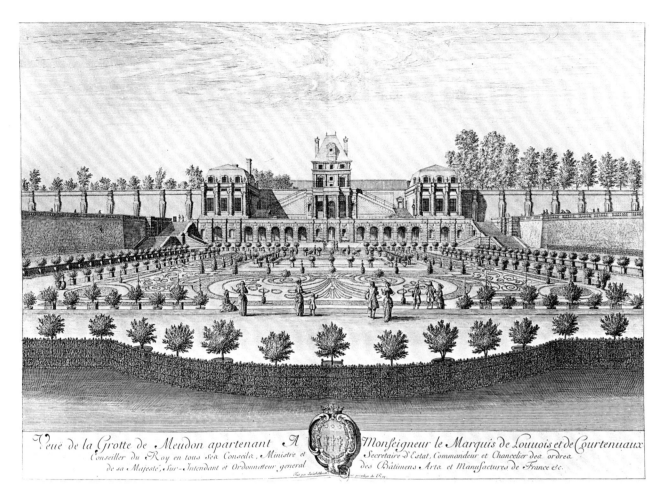

THE GROTTO AT MEUDON DESIGNED BY PRIMATICCIO. AFTER 1552.
PRINT BY ISRAEL SILVESTRE. BIBLIOTHÈQUE NATIONALE, PARIS.

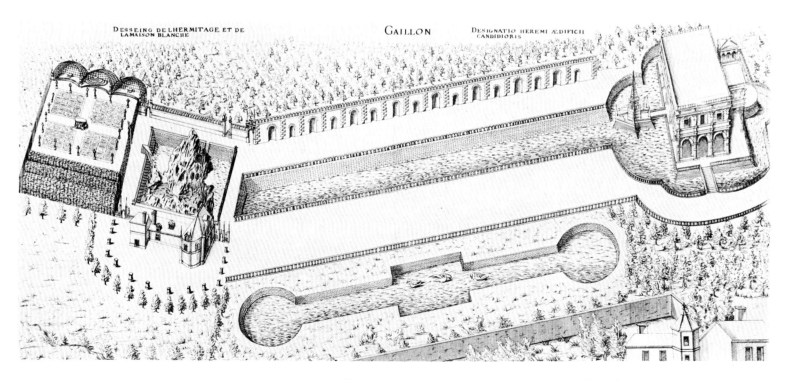

JACQUES ANDROUET DU CERCEAU, "LES PLUS EXCELLENTS BASTIMENTS DE FRANCE," 1576:
THE MAISON BLANCHE AND THE CASINO DE LA GROTTE AT THE CHÂTEAU DE GAILLON. INSTITUT D'ART, PARIS.

THE STRANGENESS
OF LIVING THINGS

The Renaissance invented hardly any new tools or instruments to facilitate its eager exploration of nature. But its love of the marvelous was combined with a sense of the concrete in a way that led to unexpected and sometimes fruitful results. Many commonplace examples might be cited. The use of the magnifying glass, in other words of lenses, had been known since the thirteenth century, if not earlier. Only it had escaped the notice of the men of science, and no practical or beneficial use had been made of it. For the scholastic philosopher (and the scholastic tradition continued down to the seventeenth century) lenses were nothing but playthings, regarded with mistrust rather than interest because they distort vision and deceive the senses.

One man, however, seems to have glimpsed some of the possibilities of the lens in the sixteenth century—Giambattista della Porta, one of the most adventurous spirits of the age. Of him, it has been aptly said that "he inquired eagerly into anything that had an air of novelty or mystery... In lenses he saw one of these fine mysteries" (Vasco Ronchi, 1962). In his *Magia Naturalis* (new edition of 1589) Della Porta brings lenses into his discussion of "objects of magic." This reference to them may well have had some connection with the manufacture of an optical glass in the very next year, 1590. The practical application of this instrument led to observation of the stars, and ultimately to Galileo's discoveries. Non-scientific preoccupations, still strong, alternately stimulated and impeded the advance of knowledge.

From its long lingering in pseudo-scientific byways, science gained in the end. It was perhaps a necessary prelude, for through its passion for collecting and cataloguing oddities, pseudo-science went far to define the relations between the world of

experience and visible phenomena—in other words portrayable phenomena. In 1586 Della Porta published a three-volume treatise, *De humana Physiognomonia*. It comprises a full and methodical survey of human-animal analogies, whose origins and scope have recently been analysed. Every facet of the human countenance connotes a characteristic that can be interpreted in terms of its animal counterpart: "When you see someone with the little eyes of a snake, guinea-pig, monkey or fox, you will know that he is wily and wicked. The eyes of a sheep signify loose morals, of a stag, intelligence, of a donkey, madness..." In the end one arrives at the ox-man or the lion-man, each being identified by certain anatomical affinities with the animal and the "moralizing" inferences to be drawn from them (J. Baltrusaitis).

Sixteenth-century scientists, with the incredible intellectual energy they devoted to pinning down, classifying and describing the phenomena of nature, never ran dry of ideas or interpretative systems. It was not from a dearth of associations but rather from their prolixity that the apparent confusion of Renaissance knowledge ensued. Its somewhat jumbled categories were offset by what might be called the remarkable quality of "reportage," whereby many forms of animal and vegetable life were for the first time accurately delineated. In many sixteenth-century monographs, duly renowned for their descriptive objectivity, one can detect traces of an inclination to fantasy that must be set down as "aberrations" (J. Baltrusaitis). Nonetheless, their precision of detail and vivid illustrations lent them a fresh and lasting authority.

Della Porta gave the "science" of animal physiognomy a new lease of life. Let us take the case of Ulisse Aldovrandi of Bologna, a notable scholar who bequeathed an extraordinary collection to his native town. In 1599, at the age of seventy-seven, he produced the first volume of his *Historia animalium,* an outline of natural history whose sequel was published by his pupils. Buffon was severely critical of this indefatigable writer who thought it his duty to set down everything that had been said by the ancients and moderns about each animal. Certainly he did little to improve methodology, the expert's main objective, but his powers of description and illustration were phenomenal. Aldovrandi spent large sums on the employment of such painters as Ligozzi, Pastorini and many others, for he always aimed at presenting the world of nature as a compendium of marvelous objects and shapes. In one of his books, a "History of Monsters," he devoted a long chapter to the figurative properties of marble, in other words, to the figures and strange landscapes traced by the veining: dendrites, anthropomorphites, polymorphites... One need hardly add that such *curiosa* had long since found a place in collectors' cabinets, along with nautiluses, flies in amber, stuffed crocodiles and Egyptian figurines. It was a fashion that had its votaries throughout Italy and as far afield as Paris and Prague (the Emperor Rudolph II was a conspicuous adherent).

Modern science stands in total contrast to these extravagant, gossipy compilations, which have little relation to what we mean today by exact knowledge. Yet there is charm, even real interest in the outlook of the sixteenth century inasmuch as it sprang from a keen awareness of the *unity* of nature. Phenomena were never described in isolation from the men who observed them. The stock of tradition that was built up, more or less credulously, around every species and every creature connected it with the special experience of that most vital of all creatures, Man himself. This connection, irrational though it remained despite attempts to define it more lucidly, gives us a remarkable insight into a state of affairs whereby Man existed in reciprocity with his environment. This is what illustration often reveals so admirably. The latter is full of significance and is the key to all such undertakings by the Renaissance, whose best work in this field has not been sufficiently investigated.

Illustration found its most vigorous expression in the analysis of the human body. During that part of the Renaissance which ended with Raphael and Michelangelo, the study of anatomy, closely bound up with that of the organism's expressive forms, was left almost entirely to artists. It developed through the medium of drawing, which was not countenanced by the universities, still obedient to Galen and his "scientific" nomenclature.

Thus until as late as 1514, when Berengario da Carpi published his *Isagogae breves,* higher education neither knew nor wished to know anything of the techniques of illustration. They were sharply brought to their senses by a revolution which proved that knowledge and the image were interrelated. Vesalius' work *De humani corporis fabrica* (1543) was remarkable in three ways. For the first time Galenic nomenclature was attacked head-on as being erroneous and incompatible with a large number of observations. Secondly, these observations were recorded in the celebrated woodcuts which, before they had given the work its renown, were witheringly disparaged by the Scholiasts as being trumpery advertisements, unworthy of a man of science. Thirdly, the plates were presented in a spectacular manner, conducive both to study and to a kind of meditation on the human organism. There is no doubt that the layout was due to Vesalius himself who, as a skilled draftsman, supervised the work, which was probably carried out by Calcar, a Northerner who around 1536 was one of Titian's associates. Each plate is framed either by a pattern of classical or modern design or by a gruesome scene whose meaning is set forth in a funerary inscription.

The illustrations, therefore, gravitated towards either of two representational poles; on the one hand plastic beauty obeying classical canons and the theories of proportion, on the other the moral ineluctability of death, which the anatomist must confront without flinching. It is remarkable how consistently the plates reflect this twofold attraction. The anatomist's model was supplied by classical sculptors and the detailed reproductions of the internal organs were placed within torsos ostensibly derived from the famous torso of the Belvedere. In this way the perfection and permanence of the human body were reiterated. At the same time awareness of death was no less plainly stated in the twisted attitudes of skeletons and flayed anatomical figures. The physical demonstration was, as it were, continuously framed by a sermon on human evanescence and the inevitability of death. Scientific teaching lent itself readily to portrayal as a gigantic *memento mori,* which itself was consciously presented as an ingredient of learning.

This curious "moralizing" feature is only exceptional in Vesalius' treatise by reason of the skill with which it was carried out. It is, in fact, almost a commonplace in the enormous output of illustrated manuals of a similar kind, whose plates and frontispieces nearly always embody the two emotions in their pictorial frames; wonder at the beauty—or quaintness—of the anatomical specimen, which was often exhibited as a *curiosum,* and horror at the sudden snapping of life's thread, which was implicit in the very science of which the living man was here the object. The skeleton assumed a twofold significance, as a schematic structure and a moral emblem.

The base on which a torso or a skull was mounted, in the guise of an abstract sculpture, bore the inscription *homo bulla.* At the end of the century the frontispiece to the works of Casserius, a big collection of copperplate engravings of the sense organs, notably of the organs of hearing, in which the delineation achieved an unusual degree of accuracy, consisted of this same symbolic design.

Thus the illustration, which was the principal vehicle for the new scientific knowledge, was naturally converted into a symbol. Yet again one finds that learning was indistinguishable from artistic conception, filled with ethical overtones and allied to a principle of unity. It would seem that the sixteenth century refused to carry scientific inquiry to a point where it would be divorced from the men who practised it.

In the handling of the human body, which was now better understood than ever before, the success of the Mannerist approach raised a rather embarrassing problem. It had nothing to do with Raphael, Correggio and Titian, for whom Diana still possessed the beauty of Venus. It stemmed rather from the figures of Michelangelo: the muscular forms of Night *and* Dawn *on the Medici tombs, or those of Venus in the cartoons used by Pontormo, obviously derive from the male model. It was the male nude that went to shape the new conception of the human figure. Venus lost her femininity, her matronly or maternal attributes, to acquire a sturdy muscular frame or, at best, an elegance of line that gives her the air of an athlete. The change can already be seen in Tintoretto. But it occurs too on a very different register, where the same type appears as a remote and lifeless shape; a sort of mask, disdainful or smiling, looks out from a tiny head at the top of an enormous body. Emphasis is laid on the rare ornaments of the nude figure: an intricate hair-do or a jewel of price, which throw into relief the singularity of the forms and the smoothness of the contours. Parmigianino pioneered this type of figure in his Madonnas of the 1530s. It was taken up in secular art everywhere and abundantly exploited, in three cases in particular, which may be listed in reverse order the better to bring out their continuity and the recurrence of fashions: the sophisticated style of the last generation of the sixteenth century centered on Spranger; the Florentine school of the 1560s, dominated by the over-suave statuary of Giovanni da Bologna and Tribolo; and, from the 1540s on, the Fontainebleau masters. For it was through Fontainebleau, in the 1540s, that the Mannerist modes of Rome and Central Italy made their way northward and crystallized around certain models that give this time and place a special importance: in this episode Primaticcio plays a more influential part than Rosso. His elegant and exquisite touch delighted a court keenly responsive to the charm of fashionable forms, and prints did the rest. In any case, the new canon was very soon a great success, giving rise in its turn to a new type of figure, the Venus-nymph, which gained currency throughout Europe. It was taken up with alacrity by sculptors, and Jean Goujon rendered it unforgettably in his bas-reliefs, before Ammanati and Adriaen de Vries, who treated it in the stylized arabesques of bronze and marble.*

(?) GIULIO ROMANO (1499-1546). THE LOVERS, 1540. HERMITAGE, LENINGRAD.

MAERTEN VAN HEEMSKERCK (1498-1574). VENUS AND CUPID, 1545. WALLRAF RICHARTZ-MUSEUM, COLOGNE.

TITIAN (ABOUT 1489/1490-1576). DIANA AND ACTAEON, 1556-1559.
COLLECTION OF THE DUKE OF SUTHERLAND. ON LOAN TO THE NATIONAL GALLERY OF SCOTLAND, EDINBURGH.

PAOLO VERONESE (1528-1588). MARS AND VENUS UNITED BY LOVE, 1576-1584.
THE METROPOLITAN MUSEUM OF ART, NEW YORK. KENNEDY FUND, 1910.

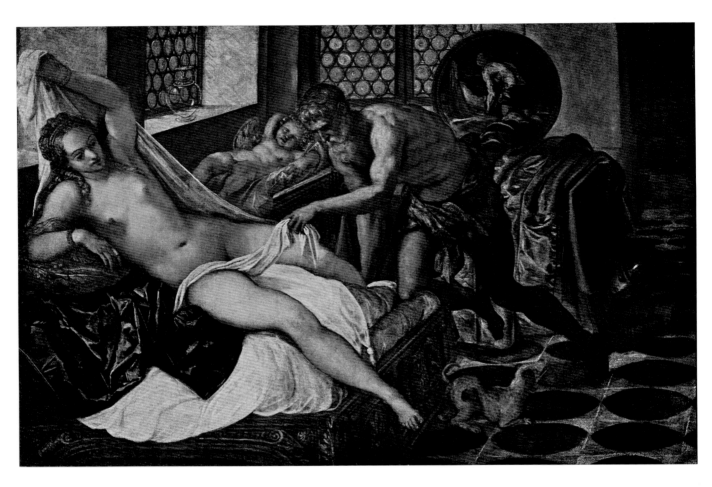

TINTORETTO (1518-1594). MARS AND VENUS SURPRISED BY VULCAN, ABOUT 1550. ALTE PINAKOTHEK, MUNICH.

JACOPO ZUCCHI (ABOUT 1542-1590). CUPID AND PSYCHE, 1589. GALLERIA BORGHESE, ROME.

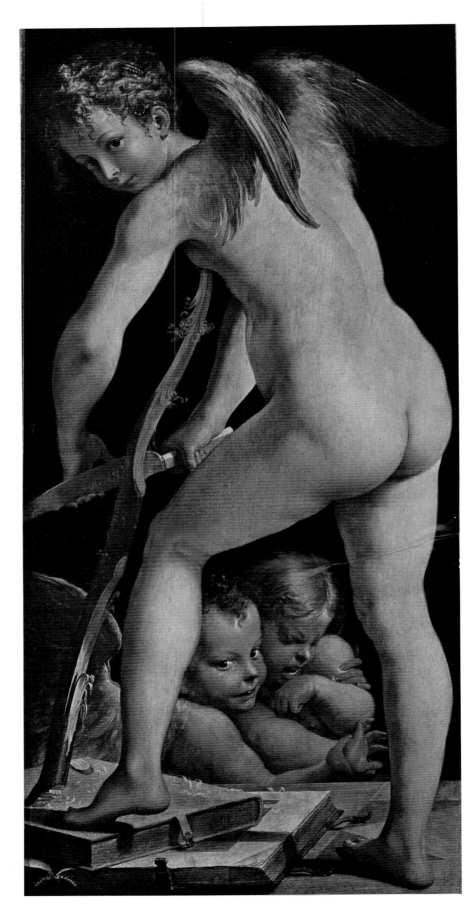

PARMIGIANINO (1503-1540). CUPID CARVING HIS BOW. UNDATED. KUNSTHISTORISCHES MUSEUM, VIENNA.

THE EROS OF FRIGID BEAUTY

Titian's luscious Venuses did not play so great a part in the sixteenth century as is often supposed. In Northern Italy, it is true, his bold modeling, warm flesh-tints and adroitly colored hair in the Venetian manner held the field until they were superseded by the Parmesan reaction in favor of a more "elegant" style. This with the help of engravings led to slenderer, more willowy figures with creamy flesh. Such was the manner adopted by Tintoretto in his *Susanna* (Vienna), *Potiphar's Wife* (Prado) and that curiously wry composition, delectable and yet ironic, his *Mars and Venus* (Munich). Veronese, however, rejected the Mannerist vogue and generally preferred the earlier type of nude, treated however in a smoother, more ornate manner.

Real creativeness was comparatively rare in such a well-ploughed field, since the opportunities for dragging in Venus were endless. She could be seen sculpted in gardens and houses as the goddess of Love; she appeared in scenes from mythology; she figured yet again in the usual hackneyed allegories of the gods. There is a close connection between this iconography of Venus and the tedious fashion for monographs *de amore* and discourses on love, which extends from Leo the Hebrew to Giordano Bruno, from Bembo to Tasso, with ramifications in the literature of every country. What should really be emphasized, however, is the ambiguousness underlying all this sentiment.

The sixteenth century was far from chaste. It tended towards the extravagantly Epicurean in Ronsard and the *livrets de folastrie*, in Aretino's pornography, in licentious plays of every kind and the gross ribaldries of Rabelais. Much the same was true of painting, as may be seen conspicuously in the case of Giulio Romano and Marcantonio. Most products of the sixteenth century were marked by a frank zest for living, which lent them an air of straightforward robustness, devoid of shame or embarrassment. Love and lechery alike were enjoyed with a candor against which the Christian conscience waged ceaseless and unsuccessful war. The men of that age, even the most lofty-minded, did not know what vulgarity meant. One should not on that account assume that their passion was always prurient and coarse. Though she may be frowned on by puritans, there is no more striking case of the very contrary than that of Marguerite de Navarre, the merry author of the *Heptameron* and the mystical effusions of the *Navire*. The theory of love current among the educated classes maintained that there was no fundamental dichotomy between flesh and spirit. Contemporary writers persisted in tracing the instincts common to both. Venus, the divinity of natural energy, was also the symbol of universal power. How, then, could a man achieve the supreme fulfilment and carry out the divine purpose unless he were acquainted with her?

There is no room here to unravel the intricacies of this outlook or to pinpoint all the analogies so freely drawn between the various categories of reality, by whose reversibility artists were constantly obsessed, as may be seen in the masterpieces of Ronsard and Shakespeare. How could a painter like Correggio reconcile the almost physical sensuousness and tactile pleasure of which he was a past master with the marvelous iridescence, likewise physically appealing, of his heavenly visions? Even when he set himself, in the convent of San Paolo, to extol virtue for a cultivated abbess, he achieved a bewitching grace that can hardly be distinguished from a lower order of pleasure. After all, even for those familiar with the *Song of Songs*, whose sensuality the Reformers tried to water down, what could be more disturbing, as we have had occasion to recall, than the mystical language of St Teresa of Avila? The vocabulary of sacred love and that of profane love kept overlapping. In the image of the naked body, so often represented in sixteenth-century art, there is a constant intermingling of naturalism and symbolism, whether the nude is resorted to as being appropriate to piety, truth and the chaste virtues, or whether it designates lasciviousness, or simply Beauty, which the beholder is left to interpret as his feelings move him. The possibilities of the subject seemed to have been exhausted when in the 1550s there occurred two developments which gave a more sophisticated turn to the Fontainebleau style: firstly, the success of the allegorical portrait, lately imported from Italy; secondly, an unexpected variant of Mannerist elegance in the shape of a coldly beautiful Eros symbolized by Diana.

There are good grounds for believing that the lengthy reign of Henry II's mistress, Diane de Poitiers, was decisive in bringing about this aesthetic change. Its importance for us resides in the fact that the advent of this type of anti-Venus coincided with a period of French art that was both classical, sensuous and uncompromising. The lovely Diana's career consummated the triumph of a proud, statuesque comeliness, maintained by exercise, cold baths and riding—by the very activities, in fact, that one would ascribe to the chaste huntress of mythology. For twelve years the French court was dazzled by the flawless purity of her majestic beauty, and there were many gossips and satirists who accounted for its amazing preservation by the more or less magical artifices of her toilette. To most of Henry's contemporaries, friends and enemies alike, his besotted adoration of her smelt of witchcraft. At all events, it would be no exaggeration to say that she held him in thrall. Her creamy complexion and majestic demeanor exerted their fascination amid a slightly incongruous display of widow's weeds. Henry adopted her colors, blue and black; her badge, a tomb with an arrow issuant, was to be seen everywhere; her bereavement was ostentatiously recalled in the votive inscription beneath the statue of her husband, de Brézé, on the upper façade of the Château d'Anet. Never were impediments, difficulties or inaccessibility more severely underlined.

Henry II's court delighted in exploring the many attributes offered by classical tradition. The unchallenged supremacy of his mistress made possible the most detailed personification of the goddess, with all the legends and properties pertaining to her. There were, in effect, three elements in the "Diana complex" of the Renaissance: firstly the nymph's nakedness, which was the chaste nudity of virgin huntresses and young maidens attending the demure goddess at her ablutions; secondly the countryside, with its fountains, thickets and leafy bowers, conveying a heady, irresistible freshness, a Pan-like emotion, but controlled and withdrawn; lastly, the sublimation of the hunt and its bloody revels in scenes depicting the flight and defence of beauty and the punishment of lust. There were frequent changes in the emotional key of love and constant allusions to the ambivalence of Diana's bow and arrows. Some of the more sensual images of nakedness in the forest clearly denote a substitution of Diana for Venus. This would accord with Virgil's description of the goddess of love appearing in the artless guise of a young huntress: *Virginis os habitumque ferens et virginis arma Spartanae...*

Apart from rather a fine poem by Olivier de Magny, written tributes to the great mistress are less significant than other forms of art. One should certainly give due weight to the seventeenth-century text in which the gallery (since destroyed) of the right wing of the Château d'Anet is described as "filled with a number of excellent landscape paintings and various other portraits of the above-mentioned Diane de Poitiers, depicting her sometimes as a huntress, naked like the Diana of the ancients, sometimes richly clad and in great state, after the manner of her own time; or showing her now in her youth, now as she was in later years."

In other words, the only picture gallery at Anet contained a collection of allegorical portraits in many styles and by many hands. The works commissioned for the château must have constituted a very considerable oeuvre if one adds to these paintings the cycle of tapestries that has now been largely reassembled and the lost group of tapestries known as the Twelve Fountains. The iconography of Diane de Poitiers at Anet must have been on an impressive scale, for the whole collection bore her cypher and included a large number of heraldic devices. It seems probable that the private apartments and smaller rooms of the château contained less ambitious works than the gallery, and it may well be that the originals of the *Lady at her Toilet* series which remained so popular down to the eighteenth century, can also be traced back to the Diana cycle. One should finally mention the imposing fountain of Diana, that masterpiece of elegance and skill which, strangely enough, is still at the moment of writing anonymous.

Here one encounters an unexpected difficulty. The works that were unquestionably done for the Château d'Anet, such as the statue of Diana or the *Standing Diana* (Louvre) cannot be attributed with any certainty; whereas those which are signed, such as the *Lady at her Toilet* (Washington), bearing the name of François Clouet, have no proven connection with Diane de Poitiers and Anet. Our knowledge of French painting does not justify a hard-and-fast conclusion. There is, however, one major work, the statue at Anet of *Diana with the Stag* which shows conclusively that the statue was inspired by the new symbol.

But who was the artist? We still do not know. Since Jean Goujon is ruled out on every count, it is possible that the foremost of French sculptors, Germain Pilon, was here making a spectacular début (Sir Anthony Blunt). The work was doubtless inspired by Rosso's painting of the nymph at Fontainebleau, lying beside the spring, which was engraved by Boyvin and finally sculpted by Cellini. It was intended for the Golden Gate and was given to Diane de Poitiers by Henry II to adorn the gate of Anet. Behind the nude virgin one can see the stag's head evoking the goddess of hunting. In the fountain at Anet, however, the composition is more full-bodied and the attitudes of the whole group are wonderfully firm and stately. At one side crouch the two hounds, Phocion and Syrius. The stag is raising its antlers, as if it were arching its neck rapturously beneath the caress of Diana. In her case the long, fine-drawn modeling succeeds in making harmonious a pose that is both majestic and complicated. The ivory pallor of her flesh is set off by a number of jewels arranged with unusually happy effect, and especially by the most cunningly ordered tresses that ever formed the sole glory of woman's attire. Diana's hair, in fact, makes a striking counterpoint to the stag's antlers, just as the animal's russet hide and hounds' coats enhance the chill smoothness of the sculptured nakedness—no longer an imperfect replica but seemingly nature itself. This allegory of comeliness is pervaded by a subtle irony, for it

praises an ornate nudity whose pose and gesture, queenly profile and graceful limbs belong no longer to naiads or dryads but to a great lady of a prince's household. The sculptor has sacrificed the effect of mass by filling his statue with open-work, and in this respect the design has an incipient Mannerism. It is best seen from the front, where the intricate arabesques of the figures are visible.

The Diana cycle finds its climax and essence in this glorious celebration of a femininity that is both winsome and scornful, perfect and unapproachable. The style achieves a purity without weakness that is almost unequaled in the sixteenth century. The sculptor's art has reached its zenith in a sort of erotic cult which remains one of the outstanding creations of the French Renaissance and may well be described as one of its greatest legacies to civilization. For in the later Mannerists of Prague and in the works of Jacques Bellange, the accomplished engraver from Nancy, one finds aspects of this style, albeit more eccentric and bizarre, marked by an impudent frivolity and a frankly depraved eroticism.

At this point the subject takes another twist and involves a scandalous footnote, to which the historian may not turn a blind eye. There is no escaping a certain resemblance between the cult of Diana, that athletic nymph, and the liking for male beauty, whether or not it was carried to the length of pederasty. During the Renaissance Eros assumed this guise in the greatest works of Michelangelo and Shakespeare. Some of its variants may be found in the writings of a lesser practitioner, the turbulent Cellini, who gives a lengthy account of cheerful orgies at Rome in 1524, where men competed for the favors of a handsome youth dressed up as a girl (*Memoirs*, I, 5). Such amusements were even the sport of kings, and indignant Huguenot pamphleteers, not only the redoubtable Agrippa d'Aubigné but other fascinated and inquisitive witnesses, have told enough of the revels at the court of Henry III to show why it was regarded as a second Sodom. There is doubtless a poetic sublimation of familiar habits and goings-on to be found in the space devoted by Shakespeare in his comedies to disguises, transvestism and the amorous imbroglios they led to.

From another incident we learn how the impudent Cellini got out of a nasty scrape. The Grand Duke of Tuscany had been sent a little Greek statue which

Cellini, offering his services as an expert, proposed to restore: "This is the loveliest, most exquisite figure of a boy that I ever saw in antique sculpture. Allow me, Your Excellency, to restore the head, arms and feet. I will add an eagle and make him a Ganymede." There followed the dreadful quarrel with Bandinelli, in the course of which the latter shouted in front of the entire court: "Hold your tongue, you filthy sodomite." A remark of this sort in public was a serious matter, especially as Cellini's habits were common knowledge (in 1554 he was indeed sent to prison for pederasty). On this occasion he showed uncommon effrontery in saving the situation with a sally which, if he is to be believed, greatly amused the duke and his courtiers: "I would to God that I might be initiated into so exalted an art, for Jupiter and Ganymede practised it in heaven, and the greatest emperors and kings practise it on earth. I, alas, am but a poor humble man, who has neither the will nor the means to aspire after anything so admirable" *(Memoirs*, VII, 4*)*.

The story is not particularly attractive but, despite the hypocrisy of Cellini's manner, it does illustrate once more the constant transition between life and the image, the swing of the pendulum from symbol to reality, that we have noted again and again throughout the century. There is the same interplay, repeatedly exemplified, between the religious and the profane. Rosso painted a disconcerting *Entombment* (Boston) in which the beauty and abandonment of Christ have something equivocal about them, though there is no reason to suppose any sacrilege was intended. Aretino, the only "art critic" of the Renaissance, notorious for his pornographic writings, also wrote some of the finest religious texts of the period. It would be wrong to attribute this aspect of the Renaissance to duplicity or cynicism; one should rather see in it a sort of fundamental indeterminateness. A final example should deter us from passing hasty judgments in this area where honesty and shamelessness meet. In 1560 Cellini, after a deplorable court case involving his morals, was working on a figure of Christ, "life-size in white marble, on a cross of black marble" *(Memoirs*, VIII, 4*)*. He wanted to present the statue to Duchess Eleonora, who disliked him and refused it. The work was then purchased by the Duke. In 1576 it was given to Philip II of Spain, and to this day its effeminate beauty graces the chapel of the Escorial.

IV

PAGEANTRY, COURT ART
AND THE MARVELOUS

APPARATI AND MASQUERADES

O Lord Hymen, who watchest over the nuptial feast,
let the saffron cape hang down thy back; let thy foot
be laced in a fine blue buskin; and do thou carry in
thy hand a bright flaming torch.

RONSARD, *Third Eclogue or Pastoral Hymn on the Marriage of Monseigneur Charles
Duc de Lorraine and Madame Claude, younger daughter of King Henry* II, 1559.

Both in their elegance and in their pompous rhetoric the styles of the sixteenth century present so many implications that an overall view of them can only be obtained by considering society as a whole. It is important to recognize at the outset that one of the mainsprings of that society was the joint influence of ostentation and passion, making itself felt on every occasion and in all circles and classes. There is, however, some danger of an optical illusion, by which many historians have been misled, inasmuch as the wealth of representations and the proliferation of forms may create an image of the period so compelling that the image tends to overshadow the realities behind it. Even this circular line of historical reasoning need not necessarily be avoided if it helps to focus attention on the points at which artistic activity and social dynamics impinge on each other.

It would seem that one of these major points of impact may be indicated by a phenomenon which historians have tended to regard as a marginal oddity, but which now appears to have been a particularly crucial expression of social energy: the love of pageantry. The vitality of a group is, of course, closely bound up with the need for self-expression. The program for the State entry of a monarch, for instance, was planned so carefully that it was as if the character of the new reign would be determined by the splendor of this performance. The country's wealth was judged by the festivities, and even the state of religion by the rites that accompanied them. Display was the handmaid of power: a spectacle, produced by the mighty, in which their policy was acted out. Gradually, as it played an increasing part in court life, display became indispensable. By the end of the century it absorbed all the energies of the ruling class. The Valois court is the most striking example of this process.

Already in the days of Francis I the egregious affair of the Field of the Cloth of Gold had shown how far the struggle for prestige might be carried. It often happened, as in Shakespeare, that a real drama underlay the simulated one. A notable example of this was Charles V's bizarre journey through France in 1539-1540. He was greeted with brilliant festivities at Fontainebleau and Paris; yet everyone was skating on ice so thin that none of the dithyrambs in his honor or the auspicious motifs of the *apparati* can have been sincere. In 1589, on the occasion of the marriage of Christine de Lorraine to Ferdinando de' Medici, the State entry into Florence consisted of a threefold paean to the glory of Tuscany, France and the Empire. Since, however, Florence had good reason to distrust the Habsburgs, the stately encomiums were accompanied by many warnings and veiled criticisms.

It had long been customary for every great celebration to be the occasion for festive trappings such as processions and parades, athletic displays and dramatic productions. According to a tradition mentioned by Vasari and borne out by Lasca's *Trionfi, Carri, Mascherate o Canti Carnascialeschi* (1559), it was Lorenzo the Magnificent, in Florence, who first organized processions of floats with *tableaux vivants* on antique themes. Almost at once these triumphal pageants assumed a political character. The "Triumph of Death" organized by Piero di Cosimo for the Florentine guilds at carnival time in 1511 contained a good deal of openly pro-Medicean propaganda (the Medici had been driven from the city in 1494) and predicted their early return (it took place in 1512). The fashion for antique pageantry reached its height with the State entry of Pope Leo X into Florence in November 1515. There were twelve triumphal arches along the route from the Porta Romana to the cathedral;

a "Trajan's Column" was erected in front of the Palazzo Vecchio and a Hercules in the Loggia dei Lanzi. This was the beginning of the new type of festivity, which involved completely transforming the city's appearance by means of temporary structures and decorations, as well as tying the whole affair together by some symbolic myth. The love of fantasies and marvels, so typical of the sixteenth century, originated in a kind of social make-believe and found an outlet in spectacles such as these.

Intellectuals who were adept at using symbols, as well as artists eager for their work to be exhibited, now had a unique opportunity to show their paces. As regards State entries in the strict sense of the term, they were usually in the hands of guilds, brotherhoods and municipal authorities. It was they, for instance, who staged the festivities in honor of Francis I, or of Charles V in Flandres. The result was that, however ambitious and dignified the general setting, some of the special effects were a bit provincial and there was a tendency for the writers of dramatic interludes to indulge in folklore. When Henry II made his entry into a dozen French cities in 1548 and 1549 these practices were much in evidence, and the local bigwigs seized the opportunity to put their best foot forward. His entry into Lyons is significant because of the work done by Maurice Scève and the advice given by Serlio on the architectural features. When he entered Paris in 1549 the event was rightly regarded as a sort of manifesto by the new school. One should not see in this any connection with the beginning of the Pléiade, for the didactic motifs were worked out by Thomas Sébillet, who was to be attacked by Ronsard and Du Bellay. Still, the participation of Lescot and François Clouet would alone make the occasion noteworthy. Among the decorations in the rue Saint-Denis, Jean Goujon's *Fontaine des Innocents* enjoyed an exceptionally far-reaching influence. These State entries provided a long-awaited opportunity for various forms of decorative art. Some of Goujon's finest works had a grace and distinction that accorded exactly with the use to which they were put. Such were, besides the Fontaine des Innocents, his rood-screen for the church of Saint-Germain l'Auxerrois and the Saint-Romain gate at Rouen.

There was an equally remarkable development in Italy, above all in Tuscany, where political connections and matrimonial alliances with France played a considerable part. One has the impression, especially in the days of Catherine de' Medici, that the two courts were hand in glove, each benefiting from the other's discoveries. In 1565 the wedding of Francesco de' Medici and Joan of Austria was the occasion of a ceremonial entry, whose management was entrusted to Vasari. He had made a speciality of *apparati* and was determined to surpass himself. With his friend Borghini he devised a mythological cavalcade, the *Masquerade of the Gods*, based on a recent essay by Cartari and so elaborate that some critics considered it *spiacevole per oscurità*. Since festivities of this kind had to be organized at short notice and with conspicuous dexterity, their preparation required prodigies of inventiveness. The keynote of the whole affair was learning and brio, *invenzione* and *bravura*. In such conditions the court artist was in his element. The statues were entrusted to Ammanati and Giovanni da Bologna; the scenery was rapidly painted under Bronzino's supervision. The State entry of 1565 seemed the last word in this flamboyant form of art—the *ne plus ultra* of what had by now become an established tradition.

Nonetheless, it was outdone by the entry of 1589, which Buontalenti staged in honor of Ferdinando de' Medici and Christine de Lorraine. On this occasion the prestige of all the royal families in Christendom was at stake. The team of painters and decorators included Allori, Santi di Tito and Dosio. The latter, an architect with archaeological leanings, had designed a façade for the cathedral of Santa Maria dei Fiori. It seemed a good opportunity to complete Brunelleschi's work, and not merely to run up one of the usual pasteboard façades. In the event, however, the Piazza del Duomo, like the rest of the city, was once more given over to hastily painted scaffolding and wooden hoardings. Never had civic pomp and didactic purpose been more heavily stressed. The ponderous device of blind arches was employed to open up certain vistas and close others. Every stage of the processional route ended in a sort of enclosure, framed in triumphal motifs, surmounted by pediments and furnished with a set of little shrines, in which historical and allegorical scenes painted in monochrome illustrated the interminable glories of what was supposed to be the history of the families that were being honored. The antiquity of Tuscany, for instance, was evoked by the Etruscan, Lars Porsena; that of the Empire by Charlemagne.

Much effort was expended, too, on the sporting and dramatic events. Many of these performances took place in the courtyard of the Palazzo Pitti, recently laid out by Buontalenti. Such use of the *cortile* as an auditorium might appear architecturally heinous. In point of fact, the design of the Palazzo Pitti made provision for shows being put on below the spectators' gallery. This was an extreme case of a function which must have played a considerable part in civic architecture during the Renaissance, first in Italy and then elsewhere. To some extent the proportions and layout of palaces—and the same was true of country houses—was determined by this representational purpose. For a long time the *cortili* and inner courtyards of French mansions had been used for *rappresentazioni,* always in connection with festivities such as banquets, receptions and cavalcades. About the middle of the sixteenth century one finds architectural plans being in part dictated by the need for an auditorium. There are many examples of this. Vignola and Ammanati consciously planned the Villa Giulia as a setting for festivities. In 1565 a great tournament was held in the *cortile* of the Belvedere, designed by Bramante and left unfinished. In that same year Vasari, in order to improve the shining hour of Francesco de' Medici's wedding, used a view of the familiar Piazza Santa Trinità as the stage-setting for his *intermedie.* At one moment the scene gradually filled with clouds, and the gods assembled on what had previously been a Florentine square. The metamorphosis of the city was so much a part of the festivities that in this case it actually took place on the stage. The notion of the gods enthroned on Olympus found great favor as a symbol and justification of earthly revels. One finds it again and again, from the Farnesina Loggia and the tower of the Château de Tanlay down to the humblest manor-houses. The vision of the gods carousing was never more popular than in the days when it was used as a loftier version of the gaudy and sometimes licentious banquets that were given in palaces, *cortili* and *loggie.*

About 1570 the festal art reached a sort of climax. The State entries into Paris of Charles IX and his queen, Elizabeth of Austria, in 1571 took their tone from those, still fresh in men's minds, of Henry II. But they did so in a spirit of emulation which resulted in a further development with all the earmarks of a sort of hyper-Mannerism. The designs were executed by the wood-carver Charles le Conte, the painter Niccolò dell'Abbate, the sculptor Germain Pilon and the decorator Pierre d'Angers. Embellishment was carried to the highest pitch, and ornamental arches had never been loaded with such exuberant or fantastic trimmings.

The ceremony took place during a truce in the civil war. An echo of the great precedent of 1549 seemed the more timely since it was felt desirable to reassert the monarchical authority. This was made easier by the cooperation of Ronsard, who at that time was engaged in writing the *Franciade.* On this occasion mythological and political themes were more closely and subtly interwoven. Thus the base of the arch on the Pont Notre-Dame bore a "strange and rustic device" above which appeared the heraldic ship of Paris, flanked by "two handsome young men, each with a star on his head, who made as if to touch the ship and assist her." These Dioscuri were the King and his brother Henry. One is aware of a scholarly mind having planned these allegories. When the Queen made her entry three weeks after the King, the whole affair reached a climax in the décor of the great hall of the bishop's palace for the banquet given by the city. There were five pictures on the ceiling and nineteen arranged in a frieze, "equally spaced between the pillars, which were in effect statues supporting the roof of the hall." The ensemble related incidents from the life of Cadmus, "taken from the book by Nonnus, a Greek poet." Around Cadmus and his wife were portrayed Harmony in triumph on the magic vessel and the lives of their children, Semele, Pentheus and Actaeon. In this unusual conceit one can see the hand of Dorat, a leading member of the Pléiade, from whom the work had been commissioned. It is astonishing to see how the mythological scenes are shot through with allusions to the French royal House, its fame and future, its close association with the mysteries of religion. It has even been suggested that the reference to Bacchus, Cadmus' son, was intended to presage the birth of a universal monarch. "Dorat must have been delighted at the wonderful way in which Nonnus lent himself to such allusions. Yet the story of the sons of Cadmus was a grim tragedy, whose characters, smitten with divine Dionysiac madness, destroyed themselves in horrible circumstances. Unwittingly Dorat foretold the disasters to come" (F. Yates). The Massacre of St Bartholomew occurred on August 24th, 1572, and the Valois prince died leaving no heirs.

Yet the revels continued unabated, swept along, it would seem, by an irresistible current. The court of Henry III lived in a whirl of amusement; but underlying all the new diversions one is conscious of a desire to perpetuate the glories of the dynasty and, indeed, the artistic tradition which these entertainments had created. In 1582 a set of Flemish tapestries, based on drawings by Antoine Caron, was woven to commemorate the festivities organized twenty years earlier by Catherine de' Medici at Bayonne, Fontainebleau and the Tuileries. Although the country was being torn asunder by political and religious strife, the French court was still aware that it had brought the art of princely splendor to a kind of perfection. There was now no question of making a popular appeal. The new creations were restricted to the narrow circle of courtiers and nobles. Within it were included, however, foreign ambassadors and observers, and political opponents as well as friends, in the hope of extracting some benefit from the sheer brilliance of the spectacle.

On October 15th, 1581, the marriage of the Duc de Joyeuse to Marguerite de Vaudémont, the Queen's sister, was made the occasion of the remarkable *Ballet comique*. Performed in the Salle de Bourbon, this was a landmark in the history of court ballet, stagecraft and music, and it was still being quoted a century later as a model of its kind. It has rightly been described as a perfect combination of music, dancing, scenery and costume, along the lines laid down by De Baïf's Academy (F. Yates).

The general argument was taken from the legend of Circe, in which moral, divine and cosmic forces were at war. New identities were continually assumed and abandoned as the struggle between natural and celestial powers swayed to and fro. Lords and ladies in the audience were presented by naiads with tokens from their watery realm. The Orphic power was invoked to bring harmony out of discord. As in the festivities at Fontainebleau in 1564, when Catherine de' Medici had tried to reconcile the warring factions, an appeal was made in favor of concord and the common weal, which the author, Beaujoyeux, reiterated in his envoi: "This will serve as a true and irrefutable sign that your kingdom is solidly built upon a rock." The performance was really an allegory of the state of the realm, seeking to exorcize schism and disaster by the charms of music and festal magnificence.

Paris and Florence provide striking instances, but State entries of the Emperor had taken place frequently in the time of Charles V, both in the Low Countries and in Spain. One could point to others, in England or at Prague. The impact of this highly complex phenomenon can hardly be over-stated, compounded as it was of ceremonial, fantasy and movement. In the later expressions of Mannerism one finds the plastic arts being increasingly pervaded by musical and choreographic rhythms. Architecture and decoration, too, were affected in a manner that we shall try to elucidate. Above all, though, one should emphasize the pivotal character of such displays, whose style was both social and artistic. All these masques were advertised as fashionable creations. The floats and *apparati* were reproduced in engravings and adapted to every kind of imitation and pastiche. The festival amounted in effect to a self-portrait of court society.

During the first half of the century the portrait had been pre-eminently the means whereby an important personage ensured his personal and social status. The group portrait, especially when it depicted the banquets of gods and men, displayed the ideal image that courtiers wanted to give of themselves. In the Valois festivities, as in the dramatic interludes at Florence in 1565, there was an overt connection between the stage, where the gods were to make their appearance, and the auditorium filled with noblemen and their ladies. One may well ask which was the actual performance, for clearly it was divided in two. When the scene-shifters had done their work the audience was, as it were, transported to the heights of Olympus, where the gods had not yet taken their seats. "The result was a play in reverse, for the spectators were now the protagonists and the actors' role was merely to reflect and confirm their superiority by giving it histrionic form. This, after all, is perfectly suited to a wedding, where the young couple are the center of attraction and the theatrical performance is merely put on in order to wish them well" (R. Bernheimer). The split-level character of Renaissance drama helps to account for its slow development and the fact that it was so long compelled to play second fiddle. While it owed its origin to court festivities it suffered from the excessive importance attached to them. It needed the genius of the Elizabethans to emancipate tragedy from its subjugation to the symbolism and brilliant artificiality of court life.

6

ANIMATED STRUCTURES

The applied arts reached a new pitch of perfection in the sixteenth century, particularly the arts of the potter, the glass-maker, the goldsmith and the armorer. While in Tuscany and Lombardy the molten glass was simply poured into molds, in Venice it was blown: this expert technique, seconded by more careful firing, gave Venetian glass a flawless transparency and an unequaled variety of delicate and appealing shapes. These goblets, ewers, bowls and crystal cups were generally incised with a diamond point and covered with scrolls, inscriptions and grotesques.

Torquato Tasso, during a stay in France in 1572, found little to admire in the art and the way of life. Only the stained glass windows impressed him. "With us," he wrote, "the glass-maker's art serves only for show and for wine-bibbers. Here it adorns the house of God and the religious service." The Italian poet probably found French stained glass all the more to his liking because, from the masterpieces of Engrand le Prince at Rouen and Beauvais to the recent ensembles at Ecouen and in the church of Saint-Gervais in Paris, it had followed the evolution of modern taste: the usual ornamental repertory of aedicules and medallions, framing scenes crowded with figures, gained an additional appeal from the more perfect transparency achieved by Renaissance glass-makers.

NICCOLÒ TRIBOLO (1500-1550).
THE GOD PAN, 1549. BRONZE.
MUSEO NAZIONALE (BARGELLO), FLORENCE.

WENZEL JAMNITZER (1508-1585).
EWER, ABOUT 1570. NAUTILUS SHELL AND SILVER.
SCHATZKAMMER DER RESIDENZ, MUNICH.

ADRIAEN DE VRIES (1560-1626). PSYCHE CARRYING
THE JAR WITH THE OINTMENT OF BEAUTY, 1593.
BRONZE. NATIONAL MUSEUM, STOCKHOLM.

THE GATE OF THE PAINTERS: ARCH OF TRIUMPH
ERECTED FOR THE ENTRY OF CHARLES IX INTO PARIS, 1571.
PRINT. BIBLIOTHÈQUE NATIONALE, PARIS.

CORNELIS FLORIS (1514-1575). ARCH OF TRIUMPH ERECTED FOR
THE ENTRY OF CHARLES V AND HIS SON PHILIP INTO ANTWERP,
1549. PRINT. BIBLIOTHÈQUE NATIONALE, PARIS.

ETIENNE DELAUNE (1518/19-1583). PARADE SHIELD OF HENRY II OF FRANCE.
THE METROPOLITAN MUSEUM OF ART, NEW YORK. HARRIS BRISBANE DICK FUND, 1934.

DANESE CATTANEO (1509-1573). FORTUNE. BRONZE.
MUSEO NAZIONALE (BARGELLO), FLORENCE.

PELLEGRINO TIBALDI (ABOUT 1527-1596).
DESIGN FOR A FRIEZE.
ROYAL LIBRARY, WINDSOR CASTLE.
BY GRACIOUS PERMISSION
OF HER MAJESTY THE QUEEN.

By the mid-sixteenth century there was hardly a ruler in Christendom who had not ordered a majolica table service from Gubbio or Urbino, or from the local workshops that imitated Italian models. To Niccolò Pellipario and his makers of painted and glazed pottery went the credit for adapting the art of Raphael to ceramic decoration. These fine wares became a fresh medium for the same thematic repertory: a figure subject in the hollow of a dish set off by the rim as if by a medallion, or intricate patterns of garlands or concentric bands of now rather tame grotesques. One man, however, went far beyond these competent adaptors and gave a new and surprising turn to ceramic decoration: this was Bernard Palissy who, with singular perseverance, invented the faience known as *rustique figuline* and adorned his sumptuous vases, his unusable plates, and even the miniature grotto he erected in the garden of the Tuileries, with an extravagant fauna of reptiles and insects. For his French and foreign clients he had the prestige of the highly skilled craftsman whose handiwork vibrates with life. He thus obtained, with a kind of guileless simplicity, the same results as the goldsmiths of Augsburg and Munich who, a few years later, specialized in the capriccio based on natural forms. A nautilus mounted by Jamnitzer is at once a perfect harmony between gilt bronze or silver and pearly surfaces, a triumph of the marvelous, and an affirmation of the privileges of an art which, with its sphinxes and chimeras, wholly renews the object. Its success is vouched for by an enormous production in Germany, a somewhat smaller production in Italy.

One field of the applied arts in which North and South vied on equal terms is that of armor, in particular the show pieces of decorative armor. A history, still unwritten, of the ornamented helmet, shield and cuirass would throw interesting sidelights on Renaissance art. Here, in the sixteenth century, ornament ran riot, and with its incrustations, medallions and damascened figures plate armor became magnificently decorative and quite unusable. It was Cellini's talent for chasing and embossing that made his fortune in Rome and in Paris. No great family but had its collection of fantastic armor, brought out on festive occasions to turn grandees into glittering metal manikins. In the ceremonial helmets and armor wrought by Lucio Piccinino, the famous Lombard specialist, the intricate combination of overlapping plates produced shimmering effects for which probably the only equivalent is to be found in Japanese armor. Here too the standard ornaments on crests and shoulder-pieces were hybrids, dragons and chimeras, together with antique motifs like scimitars and trophies, admirably set off by reliefs and chasing. The shield of Henry II, cast and chiseled by Etienne Delaune, even includes a miniature battle scene, in keeping with the urge to decorate walls and objects with the same compositions, differing only in size.

The object thus tended to be treated less and less for its own sake, its structure being transposed into a living form or a lifelike support. The exuberant bronzes of Tribolo were perhaps intended to garnish ink-stands or a scrittorio. The everyday world was thus carried to its maximum intensity; in a frieze designed by Pellegrino Tibaldi there is a dramatic tension which envelops the space around it. No wonder the fireplace inside the home, like the bays and doorways outside it, became the focus of varied, often highly spirited fantasies. In nearly every country there are striking examples, especially in the second half of the sixteenth century. The artist applies his imagination to them as ardently as if he were raising a temporary arch of triumph for a State entry.

Dietterlin finally lost sight of the utilitarian function of the object, carried away by the sweep and turbulence of the forms he imposed on it. At this point ornament became a means of remodeling the world of artefacts and architecture with a view to enhancing its power of fascination. To that end a battery of amusing, menacing, disconcerting or exquisite effects was brought to bear, the same effects as in the repertory of motifs and symbols furnished by ancient fable. One has only to see what after so many years of familiarity with them the gods had become towards the end of the sixteenth century—burly (Goltzius), rakish (de Vries), queer (Bellange). But this trend of taste sprang in part from the need, so characteristic of the Renaissance, to vitalize everything it touched.

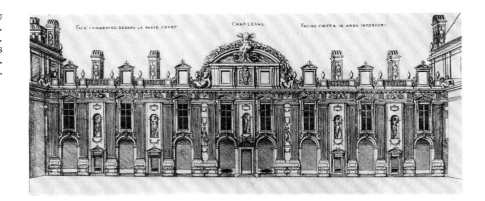

JACQUES ANDROUET DU CERCEAU
(ABOUT 1510-ABOUT 1585).
CHÂTEAU DE CHARLEVAL.
PRINT FROM "LES PLUS EXCELLENTS
BASTIMENTS DE FRANCE," 1579.
BIBLIOTHÈQUE NATIONALE, PARIS.

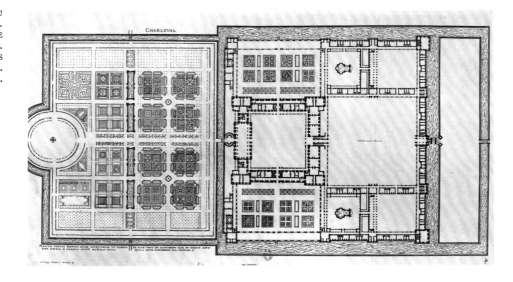

JACQUES ANDROUET DU CERCEAU
(ABOUT 1510-ABOUT 1585).
GROUND PLAN OF THE
CHÂTEAU DE CHARLEVAL.
PRINT FROM "LES PLUS EXCELLENTS
BASTIMENTS DE FRANCE," 1579.
BIBLIOTHÈQUE NATIONALE, PARIS.

GIACOMO DA VIGNOLA (1507-1573).
GROUND PLAN OF THE
FARNESE PALACE AT CAPRAROLA. PRINT.
BIBLIOTHÈQUE NATIONALE, PARIS.

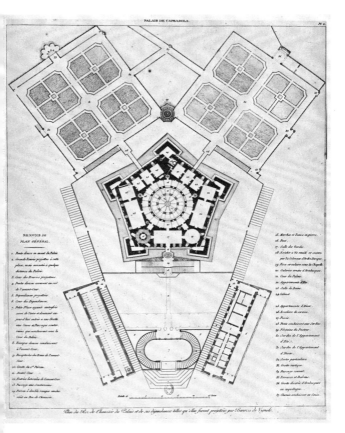

GIACOMO DA VIGNOLA (1507-1573).
ELEVATION AND SECTION OF THE FARNESE PALACE AT CAPRAROLA. PRINT.
BIBLIOTHÈQUE NATIONALE, PARIS.

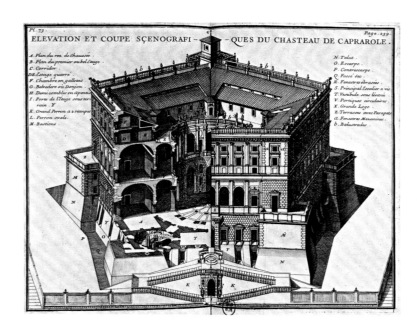

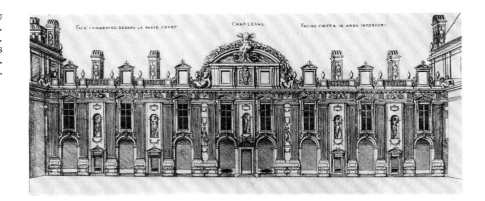

170

JACQUES BELLANGE (ACTIVE 1602-1616). DIANA AND ORION. PRINT.
BIBLIOTHÈQUE NATIONALE, PARIS.

HENDRICK GOLTZIUS (1558-1617). HERCULES, 1589.
PRINT. RIJKSPRENTENKABINET, RIJKSMUSEUM, AMSTERDAM.

THE IDEAL CITY AND UTOPIA

Although civic life was enriched by the Renaissance, the idea of the city as a complete social organism had hardly emerged. The beginnings of town-planning appear for the most part in the guise of fiction, occasionally in an actual plan. The earliest monograph on the "ideal city" was that which Filarete wrote in the fifteenth century for Francesco Sforza. It was an imaginary conversation whose description of the new royal city was partly functional and geometric, in the sense of abstract speculation on design, and partly decorative, in the form of fantastically ornamented architectural models. This work seems to have had little influence on the sixteenth century, but it is typical of the way in which mere flights of fancy developed into serious reflection on the political rather than the social functions of architecture. Thomas More started from the other end. In his *Utopia* (Louvain, 1516) the English Chancellor embroidered on the theme of a New World; but his island was primarily the abode of a new society, based on truly Christian and ethical principles. The humanist was trying to determine the features of a robust, plain-living community who should have imbibed and practised the Erasmian critique of religious and political institutions. More had nonetheless to give his islanders "a local habitation and a name," which led him to construct a setting with architectural forms and some sort of general plan.

The philosophy of Renaissance town-planning evolved in two directions: from ideal architecture to social organization and from the ideal social structure to architecture (R. Klein, 1962). In most cases it is impossible and would in any case be unprofitable to separate the two aspects. Rabelais' Abbaye de Thélème, whose fine inner courtyard and many stories, towers and staircases are so lovingly described, was designed for comfort. Its many cells and corridors, however, were only appropriate for the community of well-born equals who were to inhabit his anti-monastery. Like most visions of a new and happier world, the Abbey was an ivory tower, a "city of dreaming spires."

We shall have occasion to examine the connection between the Utopia and the country house; but on a larger scale the question of the "ideal city," as both a fit and a happy place to live, is to be encountered throughout the century. More was followed by Stiblin *(De Endaemonensium republica)*, by Patrizzi *(La Città felice, 1553)* and then by Campanella and Bacon. Utopian became a derisive epithet for a farcical or idyllic description of a world that bore no resemblance to a reality ruled by injustice and violence. The Utopia began as a protest against physical disorder and moral confusion. There was always the nostalgic idea of a return to man's natural environment, and as the stage of concrete planning was gradually reached the feeling grew that a new society must have a new setting. The Utopian writer was actuated by polemical motives, but his thinking on the subject generally lost itself in remote and impracticable imaginings. Attempts to embody the Utopian vision in terms of architecture remained quite unrealistic.

This was, no doubt, inevitable in an age addicted to festivities and ostentatious ornament. A logical urban philosophy dictated practical reforms in such matters as traffic, highways and the layout of squares. Major improvements were undertaken in the late sixteenth and early seventeenth century. The long thoroughfares of Sixtus V in Rome and the royal squares and embankments in Paris were designed in order to impress. During the sixteenth century few if any towns were genuinely reorganized, for the overall problem was usually subordinated to the requirements of festal *apparati* and the picturesque. The constant scene-changing involved in festivities made people less aware of the need for more substantial transformation. Ornate bridges and triumphal arches enabled townsfolk to forget the squalor of their streets.

One city alone seems to have provided for its own development on systematic lines. The bridges, canals and new squares of Venice were coordinated by Jacopo Sansovino and his successors. But the "sun-girt city... Ocean's nursling... a peopled labyrinth of walls" was a spectacle in herself. Her remarkable situation lent itself to planning and she could assert her original style in the laying out of new *palazzi*.

Broadly speaking, it may be said that the only towns built during the Renaissance on a deliberately geometrical plan were the work of military engineers. The regular polygon was considered particularly effective in providing gunners with the projecting bastions they needed for a flanking field of fire. A fortress constructed on these lines resulted in a system of diametrical axes enclosing figures similar to the exterior polygon. Such, for instance, was the design of Palmanova, built by Scamozzi. In some cases, however, a chessboard pattern of streets was laid out inside the perimeter. This made possible a more even distribution of land and prevented the building plots growing wider towards the periphery. One finds a system of this kind being adopted at Leghorn and, after 1600, at Nancy and Charleville. They all display an interesting degree of functional adaptation.

There are two essential features which should be noted. In the first place the bastions, mere excrescences placed at regular intervals on the fortified glacis, came to acquire considerable symbolic force, especially after the famous designs made by Michelangelo in 1527 for the defence of Florence. They crouched, "squat like a toad," deliberately giving the city an air of menace. They were *terribilità* transposed to town-planning. They were spatchcocked onto ancient cities once more embattled as a result of the wars in Italy and, above all, in France. Secondly, the town with a martial calling had, like any other, to proclaim over its main gate what it was and to whom it owed allegiance. Towns originally laid out as strongholds always possessed imposing arched entrances; whereas many historic cities had their gates reconstructed with much imaginative and symbolic gusto, mingled with fantasy and the grotesque. Here again it was Michelangelo who led the way with his great prototype, the Porta Pia at Rome.

There is no mistaking the importance of triumphal arches or of processional routes, which at times of State entries or festivities were duly punctuated with suitable embellishments. The same purpose and imaginativeness can be seen in the more limited physical amenities provided by the sixteenth century, as in the "ideal cities" designed to embody the principles of the moral Utopia. They called for explicit symbols like statues and emblematic figures, and in the siting of these nothing was left to chance. They played a great part in the organization of State processions, which were characterized partly by representative structures—arches, *tempietti,* elaborate little tabernacles—partly by moral allegories (Virtues, principles of good government), symbols of nature (Seasons, divinities of earth and water) and traditional or dynastic *storie.*

Most of the Utopians, like Stiblin and Campanella, were social reformers, and they insisted from motives of edification that the ideal city should be well furnished with images and statues. By making the most of the civic display occasioned by processions, it should aim at becoming an "eloquent" town, in the sense of being a vast educative organism, each of whose thoroughfares and focal points would "point a moral and adorn a tale." What the Middle Ages had achieved instinctively would be doubly rationalized, by geometrical planning and by these representative features. The city of the Renaissance might be said to be groping its way towards a sort of pedagogic model, by means of an instinctive realization of the precepts of the *Artes memorativae.*

It is, indeed, in this direction that one finds most of the actual achievements. Something has already been said of the painted façades, so remarkable from another point of view, but always organized like a discourse. The façades of the Loggia Cornaro built by Falconetto at Padua, of the Ottheinrichsbau at Heidelberg, of Lescot's Louvre, are virtually paneled with imagery. The city was dotted with holy figures and equestrian statues, as in Rome, which now more than ever was the type-city owing to the significance and diversity of its monuments.

The same holds good for design and setting. Vitry-le-François, a fortified town laid out in 1545, had its axes on compass bearings, and its twelve main streets were called after the months of the year. Here one encounters once more the tendency to invest symbols with reality and to rely on purely formal properties that is sometimes so disconcerting a feature of Renaissance mentality. Practical argument is never wholly divorced from imaginative implications. Here, too, may be seen the interaction of two influences: the organization of festivities which, in the interests of political power, always emphasized the symbols of the cosmos and the analogy with terrestrial order and the natural scheme of things; and the theories of the Utopians, who cared less for diversity than for concentricity. The square plan, making for a fairer distribution of land and a more exact symmetry, as exemplified by Dürer's chessboard, alternated with the radial plan, fully set out by Doni in his *Mondi* (1552) and apparently always present in men's minds. In both cases, of course, the centripetal principle was dominant, for it induced a pleasing mental condition by means of an abstract vision of a harmonious pattern—which could only be seen from the sky. Not only was the circle felt to be propitious but, if the overall arrangement was subordinated to the central zone, it conveyed an authoritarian flavor.

At this point the moral implications of the concentric plan evolved from humanistic optimism to a strictly monarchical concept. "The houses of Utopia, spacious, airy and surrounded by gardens, differ markedly from those of the *Civitas Solis,* which are luxurious but confined, huddled against the city wall. This does not reflect a change in social structure, but rather a new conception of communal life, due to the advent of autocracy" (R. Klein).

Although these plans and projects cannot be said to have been really deduced from any cosmological theory, one can hardly fail to notice how closely they accorded with the account of the universe given by post-Copernican science as a process of gravitation towards a paramount focus. The analogy, usually latent, was sometimes abruptly stated in terms of naturalist philosophy. It appears unquestionably in Campanella's *Civitas Solis,* whose outline of a Tower of Babel with seven concentric tiers perpetuates one of the oldest formulae for a cosmic city. The center, however, consists of a circular temple on whose altar stands a globe. This model of the heavens applied to life on earth recalls the traditional images of the City of the Sages; in a sense it is also a terrestrial vision of Paradise. It derives added interest, moreover, from one of the contemporary geographical discoveries in the New World.

In a volume of letters from Cortez, published at Nuremberg in 1524, there is a plan of the Aztec capital, Tenochtitlen. The great circular lake city, enclosing a rectilinear system of streets where religious and administrative buildings were situated, may have appeared at the time as the realization of an ideal model by the "new pagans" of America. The prospect of Utopias existing in these distant lands may have been enhanced by the fact that Cortez and his companions described the Mexican city as being more beautiful and populous and better planned than any other. It was not necessarily on this model that Dürer based his design for a perfectly ordered city; but the coincidence is inescapable. If civilization was equated with ritual, it could not remain indifferent to the methodically graduated cities of the New World.

One may not be wrong in supposing that the remarkable vogue for Towers of Babel, revived by Bruegel and his imitators, owed something to the yarns of travellers back from America, who had seen and described cities consisting entirely of huge, teeming terraces and pyramids. These Towers, usually cones made up of a series of concentric rings, were a telescopic extension of the design for an ideal city. Their perpendicular alignment conformed to the Biblical theme of Man's pride.

The final impression, however, is ambivalent. People mocked the confused efforts of the heathen to "imagine a vain thing"; yet they were fascinated by these human ant-heaps, these swarming microcosms whose astounding activity had for the first time been perceived through the medium of a fantastic image. In Northern art, addicted to tiny shapes and coiled patterns, this was the equivalent of the grandiose Colosseum, which so often filled the background of history paintings. There, too, it symbolized the all-embracing quality of urban architecture, with its double mask of grandeur and historical instability.

The social function of architectural space had never been so widely recognized and so energetically turned to account as during the Renaissance. The aristocratic or middle-class residence dominated a square or a quarter and combined several purposes as in the previous age, but with this difference, that it took up a larger slice of the urban area and, in view of its representative function, became more prominent. The Roman and Lombard palazzi, *the* hôtels *of Paris, the town-houses of London, were the token of a family's importance, often of its recent rise in the world. At the same time they were the most conspicuous evidence of the growth of a city.*

The gates were veritable monuments whose purpose is made quite explicit by the emblem and ornaments: such is the Porta Pia designed by Michelangelo (1561) or, to take an example in the heavier style of the North, the entrance gate of the Schloss at Tübingen. The streets were adorned with structures in the most up-to-date style. Thus in Paris, at the corner of the Rue Saint-Denis (where the kings of France traditionally made their State entry), the charming Fontaine des Innocents of Jean Goujon has remained as a commemorative monument of the celebrations of 1549; it was offered to the public by the municipality. The details of a particular arrangement—the design of a square, as in front of the Palazzo Farnese, the structure and decoration of a courtyard or façade—often reflect the conditions of life in the city at the time. Following in the wake of local traditions or branching off on new lines, many towns and cities built themselves a town hall of some magnificence, like the one erected in Antwerp by C. Floris after 1561 or in Leyden by L. de Key after 1579. In the course of half a century many such were built in northern Europe, out of local pride, the older style with its gabled façades being modernized with orders and effects of symmetry. The external design and even the internal layout of all types of dwelling houses were guided more and more by considerations of convenience; the models introduced into France by Serlio included all the particulars of a graded architecture which set a pattern for a long time to come.

It was through these slow advances and gradual adjustments that urban space developed, not through sweeping changes, which remained the exception. Rome, with the monumental treatment of the Capitol carried out under the direction of Michelangelo, and the great thoroughfares put through by Sixtus V, became a city apart, like Venice with its façades aligned on the Grand Canal, where each of the great families felt it a duty to appear to best advantage. But a particular importance should be attached to the many ventures, often ambitious and carefully carried out, made by the Renaissance in the articulation of space. Space remained symbolic and ideal in the plan of the city, except in the case of pageants, where it was concentrated around a few conspicuous points. But for the first time the great buildings constituted large compositions of varied elements: not for nothing had architects been studying the ancient baths, the arrangement of villas like that of Tivoli, the configuration of the zones of ruins.

Alberti and the fifteenth-century architects formed a rather curious idea of the ancient house, of the domus *and its various parts, some for display, some for use. But the innovators worked out a new organization, based though on an imperfect reading of the ancients. The Palazzo Farnese or the Palazzo Spada, the royal châteaux of France and the imperial residences, the palaces of Henry VIII, these testify to a new bond of unity between the main building and the wings; like Palladio's famous villas, they develop a system of architecture graded according to differences of level in the site, each part being suited to the lie of the land. The rhythmic use of bays became necessary to organize the masses, the adoption of orders indispensable to compose majestic sequences. These buildings, as varied as miniature cities and covering vast spaces, answered to an expanding society, a culture in the making. It would be naïve to interpret Renaissance architecture solely in terms of the problem of classical orders, even though the character and merits of these were exhaustively analyzed and commented on by authors and editors, from Vitruvius to Jean Bullant and Dietterlin.*

PIERRE LESCOT (1510-1578). WEST WING OF THE PALAIS DU LOUVRE, PARIS. 1540-1559.

THE PALAZZO SPADA IN ROME WITH THE FAÇADE DECORATION (1550-1551) BY GIULIO MAZZONI.

ANDREA PALLADIO (1508-1580). THE LOGGIA DEL CAPITANO, VICENZA. BEGUN IN 1571.

THE OTTHEINRICHSBAU AT HEIDELBERG, 1555-1559.

THE TOWN HALL OF LEYDEN. FAÇADE ERECTED BY LIEVEN DE KEY, 1579-1603.

LUDOVICO POZZOSERRATO (ABOUT 1550-1597). FRESCO IN THE VILLA CHIERICATI AT LONGA DI SCHIAVON, NEAR VICENZA.

RULERS AND RESIDENCES

These military men who slept in the saddle, these bustling aldermen, these burghers toiling from the Loire to the Tiber, this leader of partisans or freebooters who only laid down the sword to take up the pen at seventy-five after a life of slaughter, created the French home and its privacy. Nothing of all that our stablest, most comfortable centuries have given us in the way of clean sheets and laden tables, shrubbery and sunny halls and china in proper trim, can bear comparison with theirs.

JEAN GIRAUDOUX, *Portrait de la Renaissance*, 1946.

Never, perhaps, was art so closely bound up with fine homes as during the Renaissance. These homes, moreover, amounted to something more than houses. In every country there was a boom in domestic architecture both urban and rural, which assumed two outstanding forms: the *palazzo* incorporating an entire block of building sites in a town, or even a whole district; and the *villa* or country house, which required a fine position and broad acres for its rural environment. It became customary for the nobility to have more than one dwelling, and in some regions, such as Campania, Venetia and the Ile-de-France, along the Thames and the Rhine, the practice became so general that for many years to come aristocratic society rested on a new foundation.

It was no longer only the sovereign who was constantly on the move. Apart from families like the Farnese in Italy or the Montmorencies in France, who were particularly rapacious of land and houses, there was hardly a prominent nobleman or prelate who, amid the hurly-burly of journeys, diplomatic missions, legateships or campaigns, did not find occasion to build himself palatial residences, often at great distances from one another. Ippolito d'Este, for instance, as Cardinal of Ferrara and papal legate to the French Court, asked Serlio to build him a mansion—and a memorable one it proved to be— at the gates of the royal palace of Fontainebleau. Later, on his return to Italy, he got Pirro Ligorio to design the extraordinary terraced villa at Tivoli. Men of rank and fashion everywhere embarked on buildings, most of which were never completed.

In view of the lavish décor that was architecturally *de rigueur,* there was virtually no limit to the sumptuary expenditure involved in this frenzy of construction. There were murmurs of protest at the enormous sums squandered on Caprarola, the stately Farnese mansion, or on Diane de Poitiers' château at Anet. It is hardly surprising that so much was left unfinished. Many châteaux consisted only of a wing, or of a main block without its necessary adjuncts. Even comparatively modest undertakings, such as in France Vallery-en-Auxerrois or Valençay in the Sologne, came to grief. Fully to grasp the layout and intentions of the sixteenth-century builders, one must often visualize an overall plan, remarkable in itself but abandoned, as it were, in mid-air. Once more the imagination of the Renaissance outran its achievement.

In many towns new types of architecture were introduced, far more spectacular and imposing than the old. Indeed, the replanning of cities was often dictated far more by these new ventures than by genuine municipal requirements. A magnificent house was the outward and visible sign of the authority of politics, religion or the purse. In a sense it raised reality, or at any rate social consequence, to a higher power. Everything had a recognized hallmark and significance. Even cultural distinction found expression in architecture and ornament. The humanist's house, for instance, was recognizable by its medallions and antique busts. There was even the artist's house, which in itself deserves a footnote; for this was an age when the painter-architect who supervised royal or civic improvements was beginning to climb the social ladder. Mantegna led the way in Mantua, followed by Giulio Romano who in the same city gave the façade of his house the original, slightly eccentric quality of a personal manifesto. When Federico Zuccari bought Andrea del Sarto's house at Florence in 1577, he was not content until he had transformed the façade by stuffing it with large chunks of rough-hewn material, as if to give the far from pretentious dwelling an air of *bugnato* and *non finito,* symbolic of the craftsman's prerogative. At Rome he did the same thing again. One of the Duke of Milan's correspondents, giving his impressions of Federico's house at Trinità dei Monti, described it as being high and narrow, with a strange, concave portico and a pavilion above it: "Federico has indulged in a flight of poetic fancy which may well be the ruin of his family, for he is building something that would only make sense in a painting—an absurd mansion on an awkward site" (letter from Grazioso Graziosi, 1593).

One cannot overemphasize the degree to which architectural features were harnessed to the program dictated by the owner's personality. Insistence on display marked buildings with an individual stamp, consisting in a mass of devices, novelties, allegories and images, all adapted to an imperiously emblematic style. The result was a sort of contemporary vernacular, which is to be found, not only in the various classical orders and the use of niches and statues, but also in the structure as a whole and the way it was related to its setting. Among hundreds of examples, from the most exalted to the humblest, a few celebrated specimens must suffice.

The great Farnese residence at Caprarola, near Viterbo, was built at the end and on the crest of a long ridge. The pentagonal fortress, resting on a massive underpinning, determined the configuration of the landscape surrounding it. When Vignola drew up the plans in 1552 he enhanced the stateliness of the exterior by a system of avenues and ramps. Within, by contrast with this forbidding pile, the lordly apartments opened attractively onto a circular courtyard, and curiously-wrought staircases added a diverting touch. A letter from Annibale Caro, who was present throughout the building operations, tells us that the *piano nobile* comprised five rooms intended for summer activities and five for the contemplative life in winter. All were elaborately decorated in styles ranging from the amusing to the solemn, in accordance with an iconographic design drawn up by Fulvio Orsini, Onofrio Panvinio and Annibale Caro himself. It was here that Taddeo Zuccari was at his most pompous and replete in the rather overwhelming cycle of the *Fasti farnesienses.* Historical scenes alternated with landscapes, the whole being surrounded by grotesques and trompel'œil conceits. In response to the summons of an illustrious family, sixteenth-century Mannerism could indulge its bad taste inexhaustibly. The great *palazzo* on the Tiber, where Paul III had set Michelangelo to work, had already given warning of what the Farnese were up to.

Comfort was not catered for in such residences, or at any rate it was swallowed up and masked by something far more complex, whose effect was to achieve the acme in architectonic skill, and whose purpose was to display a way of life enhanced by fortune, power and prestige. There were nonetheless many admirable *tours de force,* the best of which show an unerring sense of fitness in choosing between urban and natural elements by seeking with fastidious precision to create in one part an air of stateliness and in another a feeling of refined *otium.* In the Palazzo del Te and the ducal palace at Mantua Giulio Romano exploited every conceivable mood with astonishing bravura, setting an example to the rest of Europe. It was by no means lost on Palladio, whose many subtle variations in the treatment of mass may be regarded as a sort of critical reappraisal, guided by a perfectly controlled intellect, of the designs then in fashion. Every one of his villas, in the context of the ideas we have been discussing, states a problem and propounds a solution.

So universal was the building mania that a list of what the sixteenth century produced would go on indefinitely. All these activities, great or small, inevitably attracted notice and called for frequent bulletins. The diplomatists had their work cut out. The despatches of the Venetian, Lippomano, for instance, show how attentively Lescot's work on the Louvre was being followed. It is in this connexion, too, that one can best appreciate the spread of new ideas and competitive feeling throughout Europe. For a long time the Italians held the field, and it was they, especially the Lombards, who for fifty years supplied Czech, Polish and Russian nobles with their architects. A notable example is the Belvedere in the Royal Gardens at Prague, which was built soon after 1532. In 1539 Charles V asked Sanmicheli to fortify Antwerp, but the Veronese architect merely sent one of his pupils, Donato Pellizuoli. Italy alone could not satisfy the growing demand. The French aristocracy soon followed suit: their triumphs on the Loire and in the Ile-de-France gave a lead to the English and Dutch, who before long were imitating French designs.

A particularly striking instance of the personal styling of a residence is Diane de Poitiers' palace, the Château d'Anet. Here Philibert Delorme displayed astonishing versatility in an effort to assemble all the resources of architecture, ancient and modern, and to exploit them in honor of the royal favorite. The castellated gatehouse was a modern variation on a feudal theme, and its coffered ceiling an echo of that in the Palazzo Farnese. The back portico took up the idea of the *cortile*; the extraordinary elegance and harmony of the chapel formed a kind of centerpiece; the crypto-portico opening onto the park had a flavor of Roman terraces. Inside, the Diana gallery and lavish use of heraldic emblems were sufficient evidence that the whole scheme had been devised for the renown and delectation of the royal goddess who was to preside over it. This amassing of detail and profusion of luxury signalized both the exalted rank of the owner and the genius of the architect. The château overlooks a park well furnished, as at Fontainebleau, with ornamental lakes for boating and aquatic spectacles. Here one reverts to the idea of royal festivities and the amusements of a court. The château did indeed connote a metamorphosis of everyday reality and humdrum existence. The architect's purpose was to erect a marvelous dwelling, in which fact was transcended by fantasy.

The tremendous effect produced by buildings of this kind may be judged in the light of a small portfolio of twenty-four drawings by Du Cerceau, dating from about 1580, on the theme of the "ideal château." A curious feature of these studies is that they contain allusions not only to Serlio but also to the villas of Palladio, especially the Villa Trissino. The French, in fact, were making the most of recent developments. Although they had already given proof, on the Loire, that they perceived the importance of architecture in creating an environment that combined majesty with charm, this awareness was now applied more systematically and with greater effect.

A notable landmark was undoubtedly the publication of Jacques Androuet Du Cerceau's *Les plus excellents bâtiments de France*. The work appears to have been planned in the time of Henry II, for it is attuned to the rather solemn stateliness that characterized the style of his reign. It sets out to describe the splendor of the royal châteaux and other great buildings of the age, and it constitutes a vindication and, in the most exact and emphatic sense of the word, an "illustration" of contemporary French architecture.

A first volume was advertised as early as 1556; it appeared in 1576 with an account of ten royal residences (including the Louvre, Vincennes and Chambord) and five private ones (Vallery, Verneuil, etc.) In 1579 a second volume comprised eight royal residences (including Blois, Amboise and Fontainebleau) and seven private ones (Chantilly, Anet, etc.). A third volume, possibly devoted to Paris, was projected. Nothing comparable had ever before been attempted. Collections already in existence, such as Serlio's, were illustrated by woodcuts; Du Cerceau set a far higher standard with the clean, flowing lines of his superb copperplates. In many cases the bird's-eye view was adopted for panoramic scenes of Rome. This enabled the spectator to take in the ground-plan and elevation at a glance; but above all the fact of looking down on a building from above gave it a fairy-like appearance, so that it became a delicately wrought object, as if it were a piece of carved furniture or a jeweled ornament in which people lived. The sophistication of Du Cerceau's work is the more striking in that he was illustrating a type of architecture in which the use of decorative motifs was particularly studied. The style was introduced at Chambord and achieved a balanced perfection in Lescot's Louvre, Philibert Delorme's Tuileries and Du Cerceau's own designs for Charleval, all of which, especially the last, begun in 1573 (though very little of it was actually built), must surely be labeled Mannerist.

Du Cerceau also left many fine drawings and color-washes, some of them belonging to buildings mentioned in his books, which are technically most impressive but testify above all to an exquisite architectural sensibility. The work he started for the king at Charleval in 1573 is idyllic in conception, as remarkable for its intricacy as for its masterly ground-plan. The *cortile,* where receptions were to take place, held the center of the stage. Richly decorated, it conveys a vivid impression of cheerfulness and princely entertainment. One enters it as if it were a city of the Arabian Nights; and indeed we are in a sense bewitched by Du Cerceau's cunning as the *alter ego* of his architectural genius, for he makes us forget that the building virtually never rose above ground.

These years afforded many opportunities, as at Verneuil, built about 1565 by Philippe de Boulain-villiers, for French masters to display their prowess and originality. Their works, perfectly attuned to contemporary taste, constitute a grand synthesis of court art and its Mannerist style. Another great construction provides, as it were, negative evidence of their influence. Philip II's Escorial glowers in scornful, gloomy retort to this jocund architecture. Juan Bautista de Toledo, followed by Juan de Herrera worked on the monastery of San Lorenzo del Escorial, which is 525 feet wide and has a façade 650 feet long of almost unrelieved monotony. Devoid of parks and pleasances, it stands gauntly on a bare plateau, the austere expression of a strenuous piety. It consists of a series of cloisters dominated by the vast chapel, the dynastic mausoleum. This is itself an extension of the royal residence, which is the negation of a palace and spurns "vain, deluding joys." In the cruel words of Ortega y Gasset, this Herculean striving has no object but itself: "It is an effort dedicated to effort." The painted part of the décor is heavy-handed: Tibaldi and Zuccari, so inventive elsewhere, were curiously unsuccessful here. But the marble interior of the *capilla mayor* makes a sumptuous setting for the strange, solemn bronze effigies of the imperial family. In 1579 El Greco painted for the royal monastery his *Allegory of the Holy League,* a thinly disguised panegyric on the Battle of Lepanto. Three years later he submitted his *Martyrdom of St Maurice,* which was turned down by Philip II. Thus the Escorial remained sternly aloof from the very influence that might have given it the enlivening warmth and passion so characteristic of the close of the sixteenth century.

THE PRINCE AND THE FOOL

Whoever studies the Renaissance, whether in the light of documents, the arts or biography, constantly finds himself confronted by seemingly unrelated factors; and one of the most useful threads that connect them is, perhaps, the idea of the *fool*. It progresses swiftly from light-hearted gaiety to the most uninhibited clowning, of which Rabelais and Bonaventure des Périers are by no means the only exponents. These writers, trained in the school of Erasmus, regarded irony as part of the apparatus needed for criticizing morals and institutions. This is a long way from the late medieval use of the fool as a creaky vehicle for moral edification. One need only consider Bruegel the Elder, with his alarming jests, straight-faced extravaganzas and frenzied yokels, to see that the "fool" motif was no longer confined to literature and might appear in any guise.

The comic mode, expressive of a boisterous vitality finding an outlet in farce, reached a sort of climax in the colossal truculence and misconduct of Falstaff. The *Merry Wives of Windsor*, like all Shakespeare's most daring comedies, dates from the last years of the century. Although the Falstaffian clowning owed something to intemperance and cynicism, it served a new purpose by giving voice to the feeling that moral values were only relative. This led to a philosophy of illusion, or at any rate to depicting the human condition as one in which fantasy would only become meaningless if it were willfully exploited and exaggerated. This was the purport of *Don Quixote*. The writer was no longer using humor and irony to exalt reason, but rather to embody all the plenitude and paradox of human passions, without reaching any definite conclusion.

In the work of these two great writers one may see the final fruition of certain attitudes that were habitual to the age. Shakespeare's torrential eloquence gave them a sounding-board in the theater, as may be heard in Jaques' famous lines:

> All the world's a stage,
> And all the men and women merely players:
> They have their exits and their entrances;
> And one man in his time plays many parts.

(As You Like It, II, 7)

The topsy-turvydom of values is the moral strand running through all his comedies, until one reaches the intricate plot of *Twelfth Night*, which centers on the alternation of love and horseplay. The theme recurs, muted but seemingly inextinguishable, in the historical tragedies, and it is stated implacably in *Julius Caesar*, in terms of the relationship of the ruler to the mob.

Among the favorite devices of this dramatic form is the splitting of the plot by a counterpoint of symmetrical but sharply contrasting situations. One always finds, moreover, a character who stands aside from the action and comments on it with sarcastic vehemence or with the grace of melody. Hating all the violence and deceit, he is a man sick at heart, wounded and disabused, yet persisting in a dream that will be inevitably belied: Jaques in *As You Like It*, for instance, or Duke Orsino in *Measure For Measure*. Where the play leaves no room for such a character, this note, essential to "all-round" drama, is struck by some monster or clown. Just when the plot grows thickest a specific kind of poetry is heard, from which critics have drawn, and will doubtless long continue to draw, conflicting inferences. It is best exemplified, perhaps, by the situation of Viola in *Twelfth Night* when, disguised as a gentleman and herself in love with the prince, she receives from him messages which she is to convey to Olivia, but which that melancholy lady rejects, for she has fallen in love with the tactful and prepossessing pseudo-gentleman. In the midst of this embarrassing plot Olivia is heard commending Malvolio's absurd behavior:

This fellow is wise enough to play the fool
For folly that he wisely shows is fit
But wise men, folly fall'n, quite taint their wit.

(Twelfth Night, III, 1)

Twelfth Night is a courtly entertainment, devised for celebrating the Feast of Epiphany. It is clearly associated with an aristocratic society, seen here at its best. Similar connections may be found in the writings of Cervantes, a rich hoard of tales in which a whole world is recaptured. Works like these enable us to attempt an overall conception of society at the close of the sixteenth century. The men of genius who dominated the age had some acquaintance with court life; but their mastery in combining different cultural forces enabled them to perfect an art which, for the first time, went beyond the utmost that courts could offer them. Cervantes in the novel and Shakespeare in the theater leave us on the threshold of a new era in which courtly civilization, however flourishing, could never again be so exclusive or dominant as in the sixteenth century. In order to convey the final flowering of that age, it may be helpful to portray some of its royal figures as they stand sharply etched against the background of contemporary art and literature.

The social order had been shaken to its foundations, but it had not been overthrown. Despite its misgivings, or because of them, the sixteenth century did not call into question the underlying assumptions on which society rested. And the gulf seemed to widen between a vigorous and affluent nobility, owning vast tracts of land, and the down-trodden mass of the poor, increasingly numerous and increasingly wretched. The gnawing malaise that pervades the mood of the late Renaissance reappears in more personal terms in several monarchs of strong character who dominated the affairs of Europe in the last thirty years of the century.

The most powerful of them, Philip II, who in 1556 inherited the formidable empire of Charles V, was to encounter, after the triumph of Lepanto in 1571, the most bitter disappointment in his policy towards the Netherlands, who secured their independence, and towards Elizabethan England, where the

Armada came to grief in 1588. Philip, rather than his adversary William of Orange, was really the "silent" man of the age. He did not appreciate El Greco, but he admired and collected the "devil-ries" of Hieronymus Bosch. In his callousness, piety, pride and obsessive wariness he displayed the inflexibility and introspection of a certain type of Spanish mentality. In some respects he was an exemplary figure, yet everything eluded his grasp. In accordance with the dialectical development perceptible throughout Europe, but in this case with a purely Spanish accent, one finds an admirable literature of mysticism contrasted with an irresistible trend towards a comic, popular, narrative style, whose masterpiece was *La Celestina*. And finally one comes to *Don Quixote*.

Set against the fanatical champion of Catholic orthodoxy was the no less remarkable figure of Elizabeth, who in 1558 took up the legacy of Henry VIII. Her long reign consolidated the unity of the great Protestant country at a time when it was beginning to develop its immense commercial power. The implacable hatred with which Elizabeth pursued her fascinating and dangerous rival of the House of Stuart, culminating in the cruel triumph of the Queen of Scots' execution in 1587; her redoubtable vitality and spirit; the harsh treatment she meted out to her lovers: all this went to make up a typically Renaissance figure, but of a purely English stamp, very much as the new flowering of poetry was giving England what, forty years earlier, the Pléiade had brought to the France of the great Valois kings. Euphuism became stilted, and the tragic muse acquired a stern majesty in "Marlowe's mighty line." Here too, but in a different key, one finds all that was cultivated, elegant and artificial contrasted with an uncouth earthy imagination. From that contrast Shakespeare was born.

In France these characteristics could be seen in a state of inextricable chaos. Amid the hysteria of religious strife, whereby French politics had been vitiated and envenomed since the massacre of Vassy in 1562, two figures stood out, equally remarkable, enigmatic and unsatisfactory: a queen and a king. The Queen Mother, stout Catherine de' Medici, more intelligent, no doubt, than Philip II and certainly as cultivated as Elizabeth, had presided, not only over the great ceremonies of the French Crown, but also over the appalling Massacre of

St Bartholomew, whose date, August 24th, 1572, was infamous in a century that contained many days of infamy. Her son, Henry III, who succeeded his brother in 1574, was the most garish of the Valois and outdid all the others in insensate pomp; but he, too, was a master of political crime, and on December 23rd, 1588, he had Henry of Guise assassinated, only to be stabbed to death himself, a few months after his mother's death.

Lovers of scandal have always been fascinated by the licentiousness of the French court. The dissolute feasting and dancing, with their attendant disguises and transvestism, both male and female, can be readily evoked in terms of painted and perfumed wantons, dripping with pearls. Yet these junketings alternated with a strict, obsessive piety, dictated by an emotional reaction highly characteristic of that neurotic, volatile age. In the end the court could no longer give a cultural lead. It was far removed from the idea of the preceptor-prince, Francis I, to whom Castiglione dedicated his *Book of the Courtier* in 1528 in the hope that the king's example would win over his subjects to the love of letters. It had come a long way, too, from the icy stateliness of Henry II and the well-ordered ceremonial that surrounded him. The most exalted type of court festivity may be found in the *Ballet comique,* whose polyvalence showed the entire intellectual and artistic resources of French society being laid under contribution.

The fact that learned men lent themselves to these allegories does not mean that they merely catered to the royal taste. At that time there was a tendency among French writers interested in law or ethics to lay stress on ideas calculated to promote a healthy political life. They resorted almost automatically to the analogy of universal harmony in order to define the task of the ideal ruler. Bodin's *République,* published at Lyons in 1572, is a case in point. The troubled times and weakness of the government, far from discouraging such ideas, acted as a stimulus to reflections on the "good prince," the true monarch who should achieve the ideal of order and central authority that Henry of Navarre tried to construct upon the ruins of Valois greatness. Desportes, a court poet, was too slight a figure to confront Agrippa d'Aubigné, who with a robust vigor sometimes worthy of Shakespeare evoked the wicked courts of the popish tyrants. There was also a vein of hot-blooded satire,

as exemplified by Mathurin Régnier. One must, however, admit that political circumstance clearly brought about an impoverishment of literature which was even more marked than in the arts. The court society of France, with its own style and ceremonial, gave full expression to a sophistication that tended to be cultivated for its own sake.

It should here be noted that as intellectual life emancipated itself from the follies of the court, so it gradually began to show a preference for history and metaphysics. The reaction began with Amyot and found its fullest and most cogent expression in the increasingly detached observations of Montaigne. One should not be misled, however, by the excellence of these honest, percipient writers, whose scepticism and intellectual power set them aside from the nobility. The mass of aristocratic and ordinary readers in France, as elsewhere in Europe, were smitten with a craze for high-flown romance. It was this, the true literature of the heart, that enjoyed, according to Jodelle, such a gratifying success with "the gentlemen and young ladies of our times, who shun the rigors of history and reject all other ways of improving their minds." The international best-sellers of the time were the *Amadis* romances, those interminable stories of love and adventure, spiced with far-fetched incidents and old wives' tales. Their flavor of catchpenny sentimentality is, in its way, highly significant.

Sixteenth-century erotic literature is tediously insipid; yet from this unpromising soil there grew the most wonderful and extravagant of romantic epics, the *Gerusalemme Liberata,* completed by Tasso in 1580. Amid an endless imbroglio of battles, in which Christian heroism was extolled in terms of the Crusades, Tasso created star-crossed lovers who were to leave a deep and lasting memory throughout Europe: Clorinda, for instance, killed unwittingly by Tancred, or the witch Armida imprisoning Rinaldo in her enchanted gardens. In his pages the smiling countryside reminded his readers of parks adorned with statues and grottoes. On earth and in the clouds they seemed to behold tall, golden-haired nymphs, the dazzling nudes of Tintoretto. Not only were his images perfectly adapted to the sensuality and highly-colored idiom of contemporary painting: they also gave a glimpse of "perilous seas in faery lands forlorn," where the imagination could roam at will.

A journey to France in 1572 left Tasso with mixed impressions: contempt for the aristocracy, whom he considered boorish, and a low opinion of French art. Italy, in fact, was still conscious of her superiority. At the beginning of the century she had been the intellectual mentor of Europe, and she enjoyed the double prestige accruing from antiquity, although she was no longer its sole custodian, and the golden age of the great painters, whose presence was now receding a little. Although artists still flocked to Rome and Venice, and did so, as we have seen, with considerable effect, the courts of Parma and Florence were also regarded as centers of elegance and taste in their own right.

A further attraction of Rome and Venice was their undying renown as haunts of pleasure and abandon. Thanks to the inveterate Italian weakness for love affairs, for "the pomps and vanities of this wicked world," Bianca Cappello became a sixteenth-century heroine and the courtesan Imperia a European celebrity. The raciness of Italian gossip, retailed by such immensely popular raconteurs as Bandello, awakened curiosity about Southern manners, not only in France but above all in Elizabethan England. The latter had become pre-eminently the country of romance and the lively environment of "a society of rather epicene young men with the soft, supple bodies of girls; of muscular maidens armed with breastplate and shield; of pixilated old men with diabolical faces and a youthful physique. This was the world of the mad Vittoria Corombona, Webster's 'White Devil,' of the incestuous passion of Giovanni and Annabella in John Ford's *Tis Pity She's A Whore*" (Mario Praz).

The Italy of comedy, soon to be that of opera, which presided over European culture, had little to do with the Italy of the Counter-Reformation, and the overall picture would be incomplete without the figures of the great Jesuits and the Catholic reformer St Charles Borromeo, and all that they represent. The most unbending prelates were generally Spaniards. Popes like Gregory XIII (1572-1585) and Sixtus V (1585-1590) strove to impose on the Church the discipline demanded and justified by the Council of Trent, which met for the last time in 1563. They sought also to endow Rome with better planned and statelier works of art. One by one the glories of pontifical Rome were revived. In 1565 the Mass for Pope Marcellus marked the renaissance of church music. Vignola was about to design the church of Gesù, which for a century to come was to be far the most influential building of its kind. The Catholic Church was regrouping its forces, and these were to weigh heavy on the future. The burning of Giordano Bruno and the trial of Galileo were to make it only too clear that any unity of outlook was farther off than ever. Here the Renaissance ends: thanks to an unprecedented evolution of forms and styles, men's grasp of reality had been prodigiously extended, but the sense of the universal, now but faintly conveyed by inadequate symbols, seemed to the great minds of 1600 permanently weakened.

The vogue for night pieces in the painting of the last third of the sixteenth century calls for comment. Gay-life pictures, with musicians and girls in bright-colored dresses disporting themselves in an arbor, were not always set in daylight; torchlight processions and nocturnal merry-makings came into favor as themes, providing a pretext for the shimmer of jewelry and the play of reflections and ghostly effects against rich pools of darkness. In the North artists like Joost van Winghe, with an eerie strangeness, and Abraham Bloemaert, with more brio and artifice, composed scenes or Biblical evocations in this spirit, to which they gave a fantastic twist. The popularity of Winghe's Night Feast *is shown by the many engravings of it (unless the picture itself is based on the print of 1588 to which it closely corresponds). It represents a fancy-dress ball, but one pervaded by an indefinable uneasiness; an inscription taken from the Book of Wisdom (II, 9) passes censure on the folly of indulging in pleasure. This is a far cry from Jan Bruegel's uninhibited kermesses. The extravagant elegance of Bloemaert's* Judith Triumphant *(1593) is magnified by the intense chiaroscuro: the fiery reds, the lurid glow from which Bosch and Met de Bles drew hallucinating, end-of-the-world effects, here minister to a singularly complex art in which the lights play around straining figures and oratorical gestures.*

In Venice Jacopo Bassano had just brought into fashion pious scenes and pastorals set in the shadowy landscapes of night or evening, and these were widely diffused by his workshop. They can be regarded, however, as but one episode in a more general movement which aimed at increasing the emotional potential of a picture by dim lighting, by cloud effects, by the mysteriousness of the night sky and gathering shadows. These also provided a means of adding a more poignant accent to Biblical and historical scenes, as in the hands of Dubois and, later, Claude Vignon in Paris, who both clung to certain features of Mannerism, or, among the Lombards, Il Cerano. The latter, employed in the service of Cardinal Federico Borromeo, no doubt accompanied him to Rome in 1595. Cerano lived and worked not in the worldly circle of the great princely courts, but in the devout atmosphere of the Counter-Reformation which St Charles Borromeo, Federico's uncle, did so much to create; and it was in his honor that Cerano painted the great telari in Milan cathedral (from 1602 on). At a time when the theatrical eloquence of the Romans was carrying all before it, he proved more responsive to the Mannerism of Bloemaert and Spranger, as in his Resurrection in the church of Sant'Antonio (c. 1605) and in The Disobedience of Saul in San Raffaello (c. 1615), Milan, with its unusual play of standards and reflections against a nocturnal background. Here, thanks to contrasting lights and overwrought gesturings which project the figures towards the spectator, he attains a surging violence which is, after all, not so far removed from the dramatic outbursts of Macbeth or King Lear.

These rhetorical devices are the hallmark of Late Mannerism. Sometimes they are perfunctory and fail to come off, sometimes they are carried to the furthest pitch of audacity as in the equivocal allegories of Hans van Aachen and Spranger; all the conventions of the period seem to be lumped together in their work. The simplest dimensions of space, the first qualities that go to define an interior or an exterior, are deliberately left ambiguous, and figures are enveloped in a welter of clouds, forests and discontinuous landscapes. The painter has but one recipe, voluptuous and sensual, for celebrating the symbols of the intellectual life or the glories of religion. The female figures, seldom wholly nude, are suggestively draped and veiled; their costume, such as it is, seems to be hanging by a thread. The types and poses derive from Parmigianino and Primaticcio.

The portrait, in the hands of these masters, thus becomes allegorical. Everywhere it tends to be as stilted as court poetry. It was the triumph of the cold style, taut and contrived. Pourbus in Paris and Hilliard in London defined the conventions which were now to hold good: the portrait became the "mount" of a figure, and the latter consisted of an appropriate costume and attitude.

A few works, not so well known, rise above the banality of these conventions. Such, for example, is the double portrait of Henry Frederick, Prince of Wales, son of James VI of Scotland who succeeded Elizabeth on the throne of England in 1603, with his hunting companion Sir John Harington.

The painter of this picture, who has been identified with Robert Peake the Elder, had mastered the art of Flemish landscape painting but, like Van Dyck thirty-two years later, he adapted his skill to the taste of the English court, which demanded an elegant presentation, a stereotyped gesture, and of course the inclusion of the prince's horse and dog. All this was only to be expected in a court portrait. But as against the lively, colorful hunts painted by Cranach, for example, for the Elector of Saxony around 1540, we find here a cold color scheme and a self-conscious posing of the figures; like his sitters, the painter held himself aloof, so to speak; this was the attitude called for by the style of 1600.

More difficult to localize and date, but doubtless by some French or Italian master with Flemish leanings, is the triple portrait in profile, a beautifully contrived work. The sitters remain irritatingly unidentifiable: are they princes (judging by the goffered collar) or princesses (judging by the flower-patterned hair bands)?

Something of this contrast between an emotional key and an artfully contrived aloofness reappears in sculpture. A conventional dignity predominates in the busts and statues of Leone Leoni; it was increased by the embossed medallions, in a heroic or romantic vein, which he added to his armor. But never were sculptors more enamored of ballet figures, fine-drawn nymphs and slender adolescents poised on tiptoe. They take the form of bibelots projecting in all directions at once or stand in the midst of public fountains, accompanying the amicable outflow of the water with a sort of amused expression, as if taking a pleasure of their own in that erratic and compliant play of forms which constituted Mannerism.

FRANS II POURBUS (1569-1622). PORTRAIT OF THE DUC DE CHEVREUSE, 1610.
COLLECTION THE EARL SPENCER, ALTHORP (NORTHAMPTONSHIRE).

ROBERT PEAKE THE ELDER (ABOUT 1580-1626). PORTRAIT OF HENRY FREDERICK, PRINCE OF WALES, AND SIR JOHN HARINGTON, 1603.
THE METROPOLITAN MUSEUM OF ART, NEW YORK. PURCHASE, 1944, PULITZER FUND.

ANONYMOUS FRENCH MASTER(?). "THREE PRINCES," LATER 16TH CENTURY. MILWAUKEE ART CENTER, GIFT OF THE WOMEN'S EXCHANGE.

PIETER DE WITTE (PIETRO CANDIDO, ABOUT 1540-1628). DUCHESS MADELEINE OF BAVARIA (1587-1628). ALTE PINAKOTHEK, MUNICH.

HANS VAN AACHEN (ABOUT 1552-1615). ALLEGORY OF DEATH, EARLY 17TH CENTURY. STAATSGALERIE, STUTTGART.

GIOVANNI BATTISTA CRESPI, CALLED IL CERANO (1557-1633). THE DISOBEDIENCE OF SAUL, 1610-1620 (?).
CHURCH OF SAN RAFFAELLO, MILAN.

JOOST VAN WINGHE (1544-1604). NIGHT FEAST, ABOUT 1588. MUSÉES ROYAUX DES BEAUX-ARTS BRUSSELS.

ABRAHAM BLOEMAERT (1564-1651). JUDITH TRIUMPHANT, 1593. KUNSTHISTORISCHES MUSEUM, VIENNA.

PAOLO VERONESE (1528-1588). FEMALE MUSICIANS, 1557.
FRESCO, STANZA DEL TRIBUNALE D'AMORE, VILLA DI MASER, NEAR TREVISO.

NICCOLO DELL'ABBATE (ABOUT 1509-1571). THE CONCERT. FRESCO, 1547-1550. UNIVERSITY LIBRARY, BOLOGNA.

HENRI DE KEYSER (1565-1621) AND HIS SON. MAUSOLEUM OF WILLIAM THE SILENT, 1614-1621. NIEUWE KERK, DELFT.

TADDEO LANDINI (ABOUT 1550-1596) AFTER GIACOMO DELLA PORTA. THE FOUNTAIN OF THE TURTLES, PIAZZA MATTEI, ROME. 1585.

AN INTERNATIONAL STYLE

In the sixteenth century differences between nations became more sharply accentuated, for the new culture made it possible for national schools of art and literature to attain their full development. There was also a tendency for countries to become more self-conscious and distinctive in their manners, as may be seen from caricatures of typical figures in the prints that circulated so widely. The unity of Western civilization was based more than ever on a contrast of energies and aptitudes, which in every field greatly prolonged the opposition and rivalry between North and South.

In Central Europe this development was more gradual, the impact of the Renaissance making itself felt belatedly and continuing until the middle of the seventeenth century. There a deep gulf was fixed between the tastes of the monarchy, the largely provincial aristocracy and the ordinary people. In those regions court life appeared more artificial and isolated than it did elsewhere, although one must make an exception, at the close of the century, for Bohemia, the city of Prague and the strange Habsburg Emperor, Rudolph II. He will indeed stand comparison with his contemporaries, for, in addition to upholding a tenuous tradition and being much addicted to ceremonial, he was a lover of architecture, "treasures," and curiosities. He was the first prince to plan a systematic Kunstkammer, in which he diligently assembled freaks of nature and all kinds of oddities.

Between 1575 and 1590 a number of scholars and artists settled at his court, where they created an atmosphere whose rather unwonted type of distinction must be recaptured if one is to appreciate certain features that were conspicuous at the close of the century. The Lombard, Arcimboldo, acted as Rudolph's master of ceremonies and designed the costumes and floats that were used in court festivities, consisting for the most part of dramatic interludes and masquerades. The inventive, sophisticated tone of the court may be judged from this profusion of rhetorical allegories and set-pieces, which should not be regarded as mere ornamental trappings, but rather as a final variant on the art of the masque. Rudolph's passion for *naturalia* brought him into contact with designers and goldsmiths who were skilled at making fantastic settings. In the creations of Jamnitzer and his competitors the grotesque was transposed into a jeweled trinket. In this way most of the significant cultural trends converged at Rudolph's court *in extremis*, having been brought to the liveliest and most extravagant pitch of artifice and whimsy. At this stage one can speak not merely of Mannerism but of hyper-Mannerism, for at Prague there gathered a group of artists in whom this style was emphatically displayed in the course of a deliberate return to the most engaging examples of the 1530s.

The leader of the group was Spranger, who came from Antwerp. He was not yet twenty when he passed through Paris on his way to Milan and Rome. He was in Vienna shortly after 1575 and he finally settled in Prague, only leaving it in 1602. His career may be said to epitomize the links between the courts of France, Rome and Prague, for Spranger was pre-eminently a court painter. To what he had learned from the younger generation at Fontainebleau, represented by the charming Niccolò dell'Abbate, he added lessons imbibed in Rome, especially the memory of Zuccari's elaborate settings, and to that in turn he added a touch of preciosity. The sophisticated statuary of Giovanni da Bologna provided models for his younger contemporary Adriaen de Vries; the emphatic coloring of the Flemings became the dominant note in the work of

Cornelisz van Haarlem, Hans van Aachen, and Wtewael. And this of course was the heyday of such proficient engravers as Goltzius. For the raw material of this art, elaborate and derivative as it was, consisted of drawings and prints; to them, too, it owed a popularity comparable to that of Floris and the Antwerp school in the 1540s.

The allegories and mythological paintings of these artists had a licentious flavor that produced a curiously hybrid effect. "In their religious portraits Satan lies skin-deep and a blasphemous lickerishness hovers around the lips. But for the haloes and palm-leaves, these holy women might well be Corybantes or characters from an *Ars amoris*" (F. Zeri). One would probably not be far out in associating this elegant delinquency and bland rhetoric with the predilections of Czech society. For this was "a manner which, designed for the intimacy of closet and boudoir, was well suited to the tastes of Bavarian barons and Moravian counts, tastes that would have appeared uncouth in the far more refined atmosphere of a Roman *palazzo*." This is doubtless correct; but the fact remains that the style in vogue at Prague was often derived from the most forceful Italian examples of the 1520s and 1530s. It recaptures, or tries to recapture, the subtlety of Pontormo, the demonism of Rosso, and the aestheticism of Parmigianino.

The wheel had come full circle. The century closed with a deliberate reversion to the *maniera* and seemed finally to exhaust all the possibilities it offered. The Prague style did not always surpass the best work produced by the school which, under Henry IV, flourished anew at Fontainebleau with Toussaint Dubreuil and Fréminet, but around 1600 it wielded an influence which other centers like Venice no longer enjoyed, and which Rome had not yet quite regained. It was a taste that went well with the contemporary passion for all kinds of *bizzarrie* and *capricci*. It was on a par with the verve of Dietterlin's architectural fantasies and Arcimboldo's comic "naturalism." There was nothing quite like it in Italy. But some of the painters of Parma, Lombardy and Genoa took to high-pitched colors, a tilted, unstable space, and honied graces; Barrocci was not alone in cultivating them. Tintoretto, last of the great Venetians, painted in 1588, at the age of seventy, the gigantic *Glory of Paradise* in the Council Chamber of the Ducal Palace. Little by

little the changes were taking place which, in the next century, restored Rome to its position as the focal center of European art.

The print, which had in a sense been one of the causes of Mannerism, was also most effective in prolonging it, during the first three decades of the seventeenth century, by means of such masterpieces as those of Bellange and Callot. Early in the seventeenth century the court of Lorraine experienced a kind of renaissance, during which it adopted many of the Valois motifs and devices. On the occasion, in 1606, of the wedding of Duke Henry II the festivities were planned by the masterly line-engraver Jacques Bellange. He went back, beyond the statuesque rows of figures that were favored in Rome about 1570, to the designs of Pontormo, Rosso and Parmigianino: sharply defined silhouettes, figures apparently suspended in space and huge profiles jutting into the foreground. To this he added something of Spranger's eroticism, with his breastplates, clinging robes and ravaged faces, giving the whole composition a twisted complexity whose effect was much enhanced by the delicacy of his engraving. A few years later the same style was adopted by an engraver from Lorraine who had studied in Florence. Even more versatile than Bellange, he combined Bruegel's earthy humor with a subtle skill, worthy of Tintoretto, in placing tiny figures at an infinite distance. In a space that was both confined and seemingly limitless he gave a superbly choreographic rendering of the festal mood. In Callot there coincided for the last time a consummate mastery of the engraver's art and a rich vein of inspiration admirably adapted to all the requirements of an exacting medium.

By the end of the sixteenth century the conditions of artistic life were more propitious than they had ever been. From one end of Europe to the other, civil wars and power politics notwithstanding, there was an unprecedented give-and-take between all the art centers. Ideas and motifs circulated as never before; artists traveled far and wide for purposes of study. Cultural exchanges were the order of the day, and every court, every literature, every art center, whatever its pretensions, owed much to those exchanges. The bold flights of genius, while towering above frontiers, helped to crystallize them by the luster they added to the national name. The long ferment of ideas, the intellectual, moral and religious upheavals, the decay of traditional structures, the passions of fanatics and the perplexities of skeptics had gradually created ties which made the forces confronting each other at once interdependent and incompatible.

Such was the contradictory and pregnant state of the West at the close of the Renaissance, and such it remained, in continuing agitation, for a long time. Everywhere Europe was being redefined. New religious and political frontiers marked off the Orthodox and the Ottomans in the East, the Protestants in the North, the Roman Catholics in Poland, Austria and the Mediterranean lands. The national literatures and the national schools of art were taking shape. It is significant that with Carel van Mander, who in 1604 published *Het Schilderboek*, the art of the North found its Vasari. The art theory of the Italian Renaissance was enshrined in works like Lomazzo's *Trattato* (1584), F. Zuccari's *Idea* (1607) and Scamozzi's miscellany of architecture (1615). But the doctrinal element had lost its flavor. For Zuccari, design, the very basis of the arts, was an emanation of god, an irrational source of wonders, a source only to be tapped by an act of grace and wholly governing the manipulation of natural forms; the inventive powers which develop it took in his eyes the form of an intellectual calculation (symbol) or a play of chance (caprice). This seemed by now to be going too far, or not far enough, and the reaction was violent and determined. It came from Italy and caused a reversal of positions which, in effect, restored the Roman art milieu to the situation it had been in at the beginning of the sixteenth century. Active and imperious, Rome took the opposite course to developments in Northern Europe, and the renewal and expansion of the Mediterranean styles gradually gained back the ground lost to Mannerism.

The foregoing is not an artificial dramatization of the trends of the time; it is amply confirmed by contemporary accounts. In the early years of the seventeenth century Galileo, who indulged at times in art criticism, wrote a scathing diatribe against the *Gerusalemme Liberata*, which filled him with disgust. He denounced its theme and style in terms that have a fairly general relevance. In reading these pages, he said, "I feel as if I were entering the sanctum of some little curio-hunter who has tried to make his collection appear to the best advantage: a stuffed chameleon, a fly caught in amber, a sketch by Baccio Bandinelli or Parmigianino." Tasso's art, like that of these draftsmen, is a mere hobby; it has the pale, jejune flavor of the collector's showcase. There is no strength of conception, only a gimcrack singularity, rather like those inverted perspectives or "anamorphoses" beloved of the older generation. Galileo's vehement language makes short work of the entire Mannerist culture, for what emerges from his disparaging analysis is the essential concept of Mannerism (Erwin Panofsky, 1954).

Endorsing the new orientation given to painting by the Carracci and Caravaggio, critics took up Galileo's argument, pouring scorn on the artists of the later sixteenth century. As Bellori wrote in his *Life of Annibale Carracci* (1672): "It is incredible how far the arts declined after Raphael, or even after the earliest exponents of the *maniera*. Neither in Italy nor elsewhere were there any painters left." He drove the point home in a famous passage: "Artists abandoned the study of nature and confounded art with manner, in other words, with an imaginary idea based on technique, not on imitation" *(fantastica idea, appoggiata alla pratica non all'imitazione)*.

The verdict was final. The seventeenth century retained of the sixteenth only what suited its needs: the great names of the first generation in the arts, the masterpieces of the last generation in literature. All that had given its originality to the sixteenth century, throughout the crisis and the measureless profusion of the Renaissance, was in the seventeenth repudiated and forgotten. When in his *Art poétique* Boileau praised Malherbe *("Enfin Malherbe vint...")* for a return to order and measure after what he regarded as the extravagances of Renaissance poetry in France, he was expressing a view, not only of poetry but of the arts, that has had a long and curious persistence. It is a view that until recently has locked the study of the sixteenth century in a double case labeled, quite inadequately, "classicism" and "modernity." It has seemed worth while to make some attempt to release it, the better to bring out the essential nature of the art of the Renaissance.

INDEX OF NAMES

LIST OF ILLUSTRATIONS

PRINTED ON THE PRESSES OF
EDITIONS D'ART ALBERT SKIRA
15 FEBRUARY 1968

PHOTOGRAPHS BY

Alinari, Florence (page 85 top and bottom), Alpenland, Vienna (pages 41 top, 86 top left and right, 86 lower right), Archives photographiques, Paris (page 139 bottom), Maurice Babey, Basel (pages 32, 33, 61, 72, 73, 84 top, 96, 97, 98, 101, 104, 111 left, 121, 123, 124, 125, 126, 127, 128, 129, 139 top, 142 bottom, 153, 181, 203, 204), Bertoni, Florence (pages 167 upper right, 168 upper left), Carlo Bevilacqua, Milan (page 199), Henry B. Beville, Alexandria, Va. (pages 6, 29, 58, 70 bottom, 71, 102, 108, 151, 195), Joachim Blauel, Munich (pages 95, 152, 197), Grégoire de Brouhns, Antony, Seine (page 178 top), Claudio Emmer, Venice (pages 60, 112 top and lower left, 182, 202), John R. Freeman & Co. Ltd, London (page 194), Giraudon, Paris (pages 141 top, 179), Georges Glasberg, Paris (page 140 top), Charl'André Jobin, Geneva (page 18 top and bottom), Ralph Kleinhempel, Hamburg (pages 70 top, 111 upper right), Raymond Laniepce, Paris (pages 54, 59), Louis Loose, Brussels (pages 99, 200), Lossen Foto, Heidelberg (page 180), F. Mazzobel, Toulouse (page 114), Erwin Meyer, Vienna (pages 22, 31, 74-75, 154, 201), Hans Nölter, Hanover (page 57), Maria Ignacia Fernandes Novais, Lisbon (page 56), Karl H. Paulmann, Berlin (page 15), Dr Wolfgang Salchow, Cologne (page 149 bottom), Oscar Savio, Rome (pages 122, 178 bottom, 205), Geo Spearman, Windsor (pages 15-16, 167-168 bottom), Stearn & Sons, Cambridge, England (page 83 bottom), and by courtesy of the photographic services of the following libraries and museums: Amsterdam, Rijksmuseum (pages 76, 169 left), Berlin, Staatliche Museen (page 28), Chatsworth Collections (page 16), Edinburgh, National Gallery of Scotland (page 150), Hamburg, Kunsthalle, (pages 41-42), Leningrad, Hermitage (page 149 top), London, Lord Chamberlain's Office (page 30), Milan, Biblioteca Ambrosiana (page 39 lower left), Milwaukee Art Center (page 196), Munich, Bayerische Staatsbibliothek (page 86 lower left), Munich, Staatliche Graphische Sammlung (page 41 lower left), Munich, Staatliche Schlösser, Gärten und Seen (page 168 top center), Münster, Landesmuseum für Kunst und Kulturgeschichte (page 113 top and bottom), New York, The Metropolitan Museum of Art (pages 83 top, 167 upper left), Paris, Bibliothèque Nationale (pages 39 upper left and right, 39 lower right, 40, 42, 111 lower right, 140 lower left, 141, 168 lower left and right, 169 right, 170 whole page), Paris, Musées Nationaux (pages 84 bottom, 142 top), Paris, Institut d'Art (pages 140 lower right, 141 bottom), Rome, Museo di Roma (page 17), Stockholm, National Museum (page 168 upper right), Stuttgart, Staatsgalerie (pages 55, 198), and Toledo Museum of Art (page 103).

COLOR PLATES ENGRAVED BY GUEZELLE & RENOUARD, PARIS

BLACK AND WHITE PLATES BY IMPRIMERIES RÉUNIES, LAUSANNE

PRINTED IN SWITZERLAND